V.I.Lenin:

On Imperialism & Opportunism

Originally compiled and edited by the
Communist Working Circle (CWC), 1972

Introduction by Torkil Lauesen, 2019

KER
SPL
EBE
DEB
2019

Vladimir Ilyich Lenin:
On Imperialism & Opportunism

ISBN: 978-1-894946-94-0

Kersplebedeb Publishing
CP 63560
CCCP Van Horne
Montreal, Quebec
Canada H3W 3H8

info@kersplebedeb.com
www.kersplebedeb.com
www.leftwingbooks.net

With thanks to Zak Cope, and to the comrades from the Revolutionary Anti-Imperialist Movement, for their assistance and support

Contents:

Introduction

Torkil Lauesen

This collection of texts by Lenin is a reprint of a booklet published in 1974. The texts were originally collected by a Danish anti-imperialist group called the Communist Working Circle (CWC).[1] In the late 1960s, the CWC developed the so-called "parasite state" (*snylerstat*, literally "leech state") theory linking the imperialist exploitation and oppression of the proletariat in the Global "South" with the establishment of states in the Global "North" in which the working class lives in relative prosperity.[2] In connection with studies of this division of the world, CWC published these texts by Lenin with the title "On imperialism and opportunism."

What is the relevance of these texts today? Firstly, the connection that Lenin posits between imperialism and opportunism—that is, the sacrifice of long-term socialist goals for short-term or sectional gains—is more pronounced than ever. Second, imperialism may, in many respects, have changed its economic mechanisms and its political form, but its content is fundamentally the same, namely, a transfer of value from the Global South to the Global North, with the political outcome being that the working class is divided into a highly-exploited proletariat in the South and a working class in the North which lives in relative prosperity. Lenin referred to this better-off section of the working class as a "labor aristocracy."

---

1 For the history of the CWC see Kuhn (2014).
2 See the pamphlets "There Will Come a Day" and "Class Struggle and Revolutionary Situation," online: snylterstaten.dk.

In this new introduction to Lenin's texts, we will look at some aspects of the economic, political, and historical context in which Lenin wrote about imperialist parasitism, the politics of social-imperialism, and the struggle against the opportunism of the political left.

From Colonialism to Imperialism

Lenin's writings on imperialism and opportunism are in many ways an extension of Marx and Engels's articles on colonialism and opportunism within the English working class.[3] In a letter dated May 21, 1894, Engels expressed his frustration with England's bourgeois working class:

> One is indeed driven to despair by these English workers with their sense of imaginary national superiority, with their essentially bourgeois ideas and viewpoints, with their "practical" narrow-mindedness, with the parliamentary corruption which has seriously infected the leaders.[4]

A mere five years later, in May 1899, Lenin noted the correlation between the absence of a militant English communist movement, the political strength of the organized trade unions, and the growing foreign investment of English capital, which is said to have

---

3 Marx and Engels (2016).
4 Engels, "Letter to Plekhanov," London, May 21, 1894, in Marx & Engels (1963), p. 583. The complete text can also be found online in the Marxist Internet Archive.

decisively weakened the antagonism between English capitalists and workers.[5] In particular, he quotes extensively from Marx and Engels's texts on the connection between English colonialism and the spread of bourgeois ideology among the English working class.

In exile in Switzerland in 1916 during World War I, Lenin wrote his famous *Imperialism: The Highest Stage of Capitalism*. This work was not a voluminous, in-depth theoretical analysis of imperialism continuing Marx's analysis in *Capital*, but a relatively short and specific description of contemporary international political economy. Lenin was inspired by the English economist J. A. Hobson's (1968 [1902]) *Imperialism: A Study*, in which he described the economic forces in capitalism that drive it out into the colonies thereby promoting imperialist policies. Hobson introduced not only the concept of imperialism in its modern sense, but also the concept of "the parasite state."

Alongside German Marxist Rudolf Hilferding's important 1910 work *Finance Capital*, then, Lenin was greatly influenced by Hobson's concepts of imperialism and parasitism, according them revolutionary economic and political significance. In *Imperialism*, Lenin highlighted capital's increasing degree of concentration and monopolization. He described the perpetual search for new investment opportunities and markets, resulting in territorial conflicts amongst the imperialist powers. The World War that had broken out two years earlier was for Lenin a war between "predatory states." The division of the world into oppressor and oppressed nations was a key part of Lenin's perception of imperialist capitalism.

---

5 Lenin (1960), p. 102; page 83 in this book.

The Great War of Imperialism

World War I had an enormous impact on Lenin's theories of capitalism and imperialism. It also massively influenced his strategic conceptions both for the Russian revolution and the world revolution in general which was, at that time, not just a vague utopia but a goal pursued with vigour by the communist movement. The war accentuated the split in the socialist camp between the social democratic and communist movements, respectively, the latter arguing for class struggle and international solidarity against the former's embrace of nationalism and imperialist war. This political struggle is reflected in these selected texts of Lenin.

The First World War (or the Great War, as it was known to contemporaries) was an imperialist war between two rival blocs of industrial capitalist powers vying for spheres of influence and foreign investment and a redivision of colonial empires. The war initially involved eight European states, namely, Germany and Austria-Hungary against Great Britain, France, Russia, Belgium, Serbia, and Montenegro, but soon the whole world was drawn into the conflict. Only in Belgium, Serbia, and Montenegro did the war assume the character of national liberation struggle. On both sides, the war was an aggressive one fought for the plunder and enslavement of other nations:

> [Aggressive empire-building was] vastly intensified by the
> search, on the part of the bankers and company promoters,
> for profitable investments abroad. With the usual selfishness
> of monied men the investors demanded that their ventures be

protected by the armed forces of the home government. Such action was resented not only by the exploited country, but also by the suspicious and jealous European rivals ... Since each power looked on war as a legitimate tool of policy, it desired to be as strong as possible on both land and sea. Hence constantly increasing armies and navies; and, by the same token, growing expenditures involving in their turn heavy and heavier taxation and a national debt assuming fabulous proportions.[6]

Whereas in 1800 Europe and its colonies covered around 55 percent of the globe, in 1878 they covered 67 percent and in 1914 84 percent.[7] In the three decades preceding WWI, the British Empire—as large as the Empires of all other Western European powers combined—struggled to contain the challenges posed by France, Belgium, Germany, and Italy striving to usurp its leading position. Russia fought to maintain the integrity of the huge Tsarist Empire (a "Prison House of Nations," according to Lenin) and the Ottoman Empire, the "sick man of Europe," to avoid complete collapse.[8]

Various agreements and diplomatic arrangements were forged between the rival imperialist powers to formalize their respective shares of the colonial partition of the world. Whereas in the 1890s Britain had brokered agreements with Germany, as the latter's burgeoning economy began to pose a greater threat to its hegemony, Britain moved closer to France and the two countries agreed to

---

6 Schevill (1951), p. 706.
7 Cope (2015), p. 120.
8 Heartfield and Rooney (2015), p. 39.

divide up North Africa between them. Thus, in 1904 Britain and France formed the *Entente Cordiale* to manage their Imperial rivalries: "[Behind] the innocuous terms of a diplomatic expression of friendship, the Entente Cordiale, were negotiated secret clauses by which France and Great Britain recognized each other's freedom of action respectively in Egypt and Morocco."[9] In Southeast Asia, France had taken possession of Indochina (Vietnam, Laos, and Cambodia) while Britain had seized Malaysia, leaving Thailand (Siam) as a relatively "independent" buffer state.

By comparison with Britain, France, and the United States, Germany was at a distinct disadvantage in securing to itself the raw materials necessary for its industry, in particular, the rubber harvested by superexploited colonial labor for the newly minted automobile factories, and the oil required to power their output. It therefore determined to vouchsafe military means to acquire the colonies needed for their supply.[10]

The imagery of the global struggle between "world nations" or "world empires" was common currency in international politics in the years preceding WWI.[11] In Britain, fearing that the loss of the country's global supremacy to rival imperialists would mean the triumph of working-class democracy over the proprietorial interests of the large capitalists and landowners around which society was organized, leading statesmen and intellectuals envisaged a Greater Britain, an imperial union linking the British Empire to

9 Cobban (1965), p. 97.
10 Pauwels (2016), p. 89.
11 Eley (2015), p. 36.

the white settler colonies of Australia, New Zealand, Canada, and southern Africa.[12]

In Germany, advocacy of the informal dominance to be gained through tariffs, trading reciprocities, market federation, and other less forcible means of imposing economic dependence on foreign countries began to be surpassed by aggressive annexationism. By the turn of the twentieth century, many German statesmen looked less towards the construction of a vast sea-based empire (and the associated *Weltpolitik*) than to the creation of a "land-based empire built in the east at the expense of a defeated Russia," a theme later taken up explicitly by Hitler in his *Mein Kampf*.[13] Indeed, the envisaged German empire was to be truly transcontinental, "extending through southern Russia and the Ottoman Empire to the Caucasus, Mesopotamia, Persia, and beyond."[14]

Between 1789—the year of the French revolution and the abolition of feudalism in France—and the outbreak of WWI in 1914, the development of capitalism internationally had created (1) an uneven spread of industrialisation between West and East, (2) a "contradictory interlocking" between the burgeoning North

---

12 Bell (2007).
13 "Therefore we National Socialists have purposely drawn a line through the line of conduct followed by pre-War Germany in foreign policy. We put an end to the perpetual Germanic march towards the South and West of Europe and turn our eyes towards the lands of the East. We finally put a stop to the colonial and trade policy of pre-War times and pass over to the territorial policy of the future. But when we speak of new territory in Europe today we must principally think of Russia and the Border States subject to her." Hitler (1939 [1925]), p. 360.
14 Eley (2015), pp. 45–6.

American and European economies, and (3) a North–South dynamic reflecting the "assymetrical interdependency" of the multi-ethnic empires of Central Eastern Europe and the Asia-Pacific with the great powers. These "spatio-temporal vectors" were the faultlines from which inter-imperialist rivalry would erupt in the years leading up to WWI.[15]

Imperialist accord over the shared exploitation of China had allowed for a deflection of destabilising Russian expansionism in Eastern Europe towards Manchuria, thus alleviating European rivalries in the Balkans and the Ottoman Empire. It had furnished a momentary means of great power cooperation, as exemplified by the "ultra-imperialist experiments" of the "open door policy" of 1899–1900 and the joint suppression of the Boxer Rebellion against foreign rule in the same period by troops from Austria-Hungary, France, Germany, Great Britain, Italy, Japan, Russia, and the United States.[16] However, great power rivalries became exacerbated with the collapsing power of the Qing dynasty in China, the "strategic heartland" of the Asia-Pacific region, "drawing the imperialist powers into a maelstrom of social upheaval with promises of its immense export-market potentials and investment opportunities."[17]

With the defeat of Russia by Japan in a war over concessions in Manchuria and Korea, moreover, 1905 marked a westward turn in Russian imperialist foreign policy. Seeking to avoid both further conflict with Japan and to risk antagonizing British colonial

---

15 Anievas (2015), pp. 113–4.
16 Ibid., p. 133.
17 Ibid.

interests in Persia, Afghanistan, and India, Russia looked instead to gain control over the Turkish straits (through which 37 percent of all Russian exports and over 90 percent of its critical grain exports travelled by the early 1900s) and to secure its hegemony in the Balkans.[18]

On a world scale, the Caribbean, South America, Africa, Asia, and Oceania provided all rubber, about 73 percent of all colonial produce, some 54–60 percent of all oilseeds, almost 50 percent of all textiles, about 34–35 percent of all cereals and other foodstuffs, 24–28 percent of all fertilisers and chemicals, and 17 percent of all cereals alone. If comparable resources from Eastern and Central Europe are added, as well as those hidden in the North American figures that derived from Canada, Alaska, and Greenland, only in fuels and wood pulp did Western Europe and the United States produce more than half of the world's production of raw materials.[19]

In Germany, large industrialists demanded that action be taken by the government to secure Africa's cobalt, manganese, copper, coal, iron, gold, silver, platinum, tin, rubber, palm oil, fiber, and other raw materials, as well as the potential African markets which they considered vital to the future health of the German economy. Though reluctant to commit the less powerful German state to the inevitable war with Britain over the countries' respective shares of the loot, and fearful that the masses were not yet ready to support it, state managers shared the identification of

18 Ibid., p. 135.
19 Krooth (1980), p. 84, citing data from League of Nations (1926).

9

Germany's national interest with the oppression and exploitation of the underdeveloped nations.[20]

In Japan, Mitsui and other monopoly capitalists understood well that in the age of monopoly "only the possession of colonies could guarantee the super-profits, supplies of raw materials, and secure markets that were necessary for victory against the competition."[21] Meanwhile, since the Young Turk Revolution of 1908, the Ottoman Empire had strengthened its ties to Germany, with the two countries planning for the construction of a railway linking Istanbul, the Turkish capital, to Baghdad, the capital of Mesopotamia (Iraq), close to the oilfields of Mosul. Britain therefore feared that Germany would be in sufficient possession of oil so as to greatly enhance the strength of its military and commercial fleets, as well as the efficiency of its modern petrochemical industries. Despite German overtures to Britain, and its willingness to compromise with respect to its railway project, the latter sought ways to secure exclusive access to Iraqi oil. It did so by forging agreements with Russia, a country with which Britain had not long before been at war over Crimea, at the expense of both the Ottoman Empire and Germany.[22]

How, then, was the impending threat of war and its outbreak greeted by the socialists of Lenin's day? Despite there having been mass demonstrations against it in July 1914, popular enthusiasm for war very quickly drowned out the anti-war minority; at its outbreak, with England declaring war on Germany on August 4, 1914,

20 Anievas (2015), p. 139.
21 Matsumura (2015), p. 245.
22 Pauwels (2016), p. 92.

WWI was perhaps the most popular war in history. In England, prior to January 1916 when the government brought in conscription, the army was almost entirely made up of volunteers. Nearly half a million men had joined up by the end of the first two months of fighting and 2.5 million volunteered in total. In France, a *Union sacrée* was declared with all classes supposedly united around the holy cause of defence of the fatherland. In Germany, likewise, the *Augusterlebnis* denotes the spirit of (August) 1914, when popular enthusiasm for war was at its peak. A social truce or *Burgfrieden* (literally "castle peace") between the rival social classes was solidified. In each of these countries, there were dissenting voices, increasingly so as final victory proved ever more distant. Moreover, chauvinistic militarism was more pronounced in the middle classes, who looked upon nationalism as the best salve for the destabilising ills of class warfare, than amongst workers. Nonetheless, there is no doubt that nationalistic fervour was very much in evidence across society as the opening salvos were fired.

Whereas Britain had experienced a "Great Unrest" of strikes and class-based mass agitation in the years 1910 to 1913, when war broke out internationally, peace was declared domestically. As British Fabian socialist Sidney Webb wrote: "[The] Labour Party stuck at nothing in its determination to help the Government win the war."[23] Arthur Henderson was made Labour leader and secured the loyalty of the Trades Unions to promise flexibility and an end to strikes. For this he received a seat on the Cabinet. The Trade Union Congress, in turn, expressed its hope that the British war machine

---

23 Webb, quoted in Heartfield and Rooney (2015), pp. 63–4.

would "secure such a victory as will free the world from the fear of that military tyranny which Germany would impose upon it." Of course, no mention was made of Britain's far more prodigious militarism, exemplified by the fact that Britain has invaded over 90 percent of all of the countries in the world at one time or another.[24]

Other than civil and revolutionary disorders or wars of brief duration, prior to the outbreak of the Great War, European militarism was primarily displaced to colonial areas, where "bloody wars of conquest and pacification were repeatedly fought."[25] Given that these had been of a limited nature, cheap and short-term, with only miniscule losses on the European side, but masses of wounded and killed on the enemy side, and had been widely acclaimed by the mainstream media of the day, they proved to be immensely popular affairs. This prevalent view of war may have led many to assume that a European conflict would be just as easily settled in their own country's favour.[26]

The mass mobilisation of labor and the *Levée en masse* of troops, which the expansion of capitalism overseas in the preceding century had hitherto allowed the ruling bourgeoisies to avoid, meant that the European working class was in a greatly strengthened position during and after WWI. Indeed, many workers enlisted not only out of a sense of nationalist duty, but also as a means to advance their class interests, in the assumption that the sacrifices they made would bear fruit in the form of higher pay and an extension of welfare

---

24 Copping (2012).
25 Eley (2015), p. 24.
26 Pauwels (2016), p. 67.

reform. As the war dragged on and became increasingly hellish for its participants, labor militancy spread like wildfire across Europe, particularly in the wake of the Bolshevik revolution in October 1917. After the war, European labor enjoyed greater political influence and living standards, and so again after World War II. However, it did not use its political and social standing to combat imperialism. On the contrary, for it was that very imperialism which allowed the bourgeois elites to incorporate a highly organized and powerful labor movement into capitalist state structures.

> Nearly all Socialist parties (with the exception of those in Russia, Serbia, Italy, and Ireland) insisted that their own country was fighting a defensive war. By August 4, 1914, German, British, and French socialist parliamentarians had voted for war credits for their respective governments. British socialists, and their European counterparts, had well and truly embraced social imperialism, "a steadfast defence of the ... national interest combined with a program of social reform helpful to its largely working class constituency."[27]

In marked contrast to the social chauvinism of the European socialist parties, who had reneged on their pre-war pledges of internationalism, Lenin saw that imperialist world war brought the imminent possibility of revolution. Just as the Paris Commune was born out of the aftermath of French defeat by Prussia, and the Russian revolution of 1905 followed the country's defeat by Japan, the International Socialist Congress at Basel, held on November 24–25, 1912, had

---

27 Redfern (2005), p. 22.

13

demanded that if war should break out, the socialist parties must "utilize the economic and political crisis created by the war to arouse the people and thereby to hasten the downfall of capitalist class rule." Lenin also heeded the example of revolutionaries in Ireland who in 1916 rose up not only to strike another blow for their country's freedom, but also to resist its being drawn deeper into the imperialist bloodletting. In short, he looked to turn imperialist war into civil war.

The Birth of Anti-Imperialism

In late 1911 a young man by the name of "Ba" boarded a ship in Haiphong in French Indochina as a mess boy. The ship was bound for Marseilles, from where Ba worked as an assistant cook on tourist ships in the Mediterranean. He also crossed the Atlantic visiting Boston and New York. In 1914 just before the outbreak of WWI he went ashore in France working as a gardener. For a period he settled in London, working as a dish washer and street cleaner. He became aware of the Irish liberation struggle, which he studied with interest.[28] In 1917 he returned to Paris working as a retoucher at a photographer's, and as a painter of "Chinese antiquities."[29] This period marked the beginning of his political career. Symbolically, he changed his name from the servant name Ba to Nguyên Ai Quôc ("Nguyên the Patriot").

---

28 Lacouture (1968), pp. 19–20.
29 Kumm (2013), pp. 55–56.

In 1919, anti-colonial mass protests erupted in China and Korea against Japanese colonialism and European imperialism. In India, Egypt, Algiers, Tunis, and Morocco, anti-colonial demonstrations were also taking place. In the autumn of 1919 the world leaders met in Versailles outside Paris for a conference at the end of WWI. After Germany's defeat the victorious nations divided the spoils and created a new world order. In this context, French intelligence hired a former aide in the French army of Vietnamese origin as an undercover agent in the network around Nguyên Ai Quôc. The intelligence services had become aware of him after he had distributed a leaflet entitled "The Demands of the Annamite People"[30] (An Nam is a historical name for Central Vietnam).

Nguyên sent a telegram to U.S. Secretary of State Robert Lansing asking for help in the Vietnamese campaign for independence from France. The agent noted that his name was surely a cover. Years later, after several episodes of escaping the French authorities, Nguyên Ai Quôc began calling himself Hô Chí Minh, combining a common Vietnamese surname (Hô) with a given name meaning "He Who has been enlightened" (Chí, meaning "will" or spirit and Minh meaning "bright").[31]

The Paris Peace Conference (January 18, 1919–January 21, 1920) that followed the end of WWI came to represent a turning point for anti-colonialism between the two world wars. Many intellectuals and activists from the European colonial empires were gathered in Paris and other European capitals at the time, for a variety of

30 Hô Chí Minh (1962).
31 Goebel (2015). See also Goebel (2015a).

15

reasons: education, political agitation, and also because of simple migration. France alone had recruited three quarters of a million colonial soldiers and workers during WWI, with some settling in Paris. It was not only Vietnamese immigrants; many came from North Africa, especially Algiers. In the same way, people from India moved to London, Indonesians moved to Amsterdam, and so on. Chinese workers and students in Europe formed local cultural organizations and communist party branches. Among the participants in Paris were Zhou Enlai and Deng Xiaoping, later leaders of the Communist Party of China. In total, some 70,000 North African Muslims and perhaps 15,000 people from other colonies lived in the Paris region alone.[32]

Delegates from the colonial world attending the Paris Peace Conference were seeking an ideological platform which opposed colonialism and supported their struggles for national independence. Following the conference, U.S. president Woodrow Wilson presented Fourteen Points—in partial response to Lenin's earlier Decree on Peace passed by the Second Congress of the Soviet of Workers', Soldiers', and Peasants' Deputies on November 8, 1917—which were to ensure world peace and national self-determination for all peoples, these to be guaranteed by the League of Nations newly formed on January 10, 1920. Representatives from the colonies hoped that the Conference's rhetoric of peace, justice, and national self-determination was to apply equally to the colonies, Japan even proposing a clause of upholding racial and national equality in the Covenant of the League of Nations. Unfortunately,

---

32 Ibid.

the oppressed nations were to be disappointed. Maintaining the colonies in dependent underdevelopment so as to afford the rebuilding of their shattered empires was a top priority of the world leaders.[33]

Consequently, many anti-colonial activists lost confidence in the Great Powers' will to decolonize. With the downfall of the Tsarist Empire following the Bolshevik revolution another vision was on the horizon for the anti-colonial movement. Very soon, international communism would provide the central ideological idiom for many of its leaders. The same year as the Conference in Versailles, the inaugural congress of the Third International—the Communist International, or Comintern—held in Moscow on March 2–9, 1919, celebrated the unification of "revolutionary parties of the world proletariat." Lenin believed, at that point, that the revolutionary upheavals emerging in Europe after the War would damage imperialism in its metropolitan heartlands, leading to the final liberation of the colonies.

The congress endorsed Lenin's *Theses on the National and Colonial Question*, which advocated the independence of the colonies.[34] The congress also proposed "Twenty-One Conditions" for national communist parties to become members of the Comintern, principles that determined how they should conduct party work on the colonial question:

> In the Colonial question and that of the oppressed nationalities, there is necessarily an especially distinct and clear line of conduct of the parties of countries where the bourgeoisie

33 Petersson (2013), p. 54.
34 Lenin (1965 [1920]), pp. 144–151.

possesses such colonies or oppresses other nationalities. Every party desirous of belonging to the Third International should be bound to denounce without any reserve all the methods of "its own" imperialists in the colonies, supporting not only in words but practically a movement of liberation in the colonies.[35]

After the Paris conference Nguyên Ai Quốc became a member of the French Socialist Party. In his memoirs, Hồ notes:

Heated discussions were then taking place in the branches of the Socialist Party, about the question whether the Socialist Party should remain in the Second International, should a Second-and-a-half International be founded or should the Socialist Party join Lenin's Third International? I attended the meetings regularly, twice or three times a week and attentively listened to the discussion. First, I could not understand thoroughly. Why were the discussions so heated? Either with the Second, Second-and-a-half or Third International, the revolution could be waged. What was the use of arguing then? As for the First International, what had become of it?

---

35 "Conditions of Admission to the Communist International, approved by the Second Comintern Congress, August 1920" in Daniels (1994), p. 33. Paragraph eight in the conditions continues: "It should demand the expulsion of its own Imperialists from such colonies, and cultivate among the workingmen of its own country a truly fraternal attitude towards the working population of the colonies and oppressed nationalities, and carry on a systematic agitation in its own army against every kind of oppression of the colonial population." Petersson (2013), pp. 56–57.

What I wanted most to know—and this precisely was not debated in the meetings—was: Which International sides with the peoples of colonial countries? I raised the question—the most important in my opinion—in a meeting. Some comrades answered: It is the Third, not the Second International. And a comrade gave me Lenin's "Thesis on the National and Colonial Questions" published by *l'Humanité* to read.

There were political terms difficult to understand in this thesis. But by dint of reading it again and again, finally I could grasp the main part of it. What emotion, enthusiasm, clear-sightedness, and confidence it instilled in me! I was overjoyed to tears. Though sitting alone in my room, I shouted aloud as if addressing large crowds: "Dear martyrs, compatriots! This is what we need, this is what we need, and this is the path to our liberation!"

After that, I had entire confidence in Lenin, in the Third International. Formerly, during the meetings of the Party branch, I had only listened to the discussion; I had a vague belief that all were logical, and could not differentiate as to who were right and who were wrong. But from then on, I also plunged into the debates and discussed with fervor. Though I was still lacking French words to express all my thoughts, I smashed the allegations attacking Lenin and the Third International with no less vigor. My only argument was: "If you do not condemn colonialism, if you do not side with colonial people, what kind of revolution are you waging?" … At first, patriotism, not yet Communism, led me to have confidence in Lenin, in the Third International. Step by step, along the struggle, by studying Marxism Leninism parallel with participation in practical activities, I gradually came upon the fact that only Socialism and Communism can liberate the oppressed nations and the working people throughout the world from slavery.[36]

Hồ attended the French Socialist Party congress in Tours in 1920 where the delegates voted for participation in the Comintern and to change their name to the Communist Party of France. Hồ was an active party member and tried to get the party to prioritize anti-imperialist work among the French proletariat. He wrote regularly in the party organ *L'Humanité*. For example, in the edition of May 25, 1922, he urged the party to struggle against "the indifference of the proletariat of the mother country towards the colonies," the "ignorance" of the rebellious, but largely non-proletarian native population with respect to communism, and the fact that while the "French workers look upon the native as an inferior and negligible human being, incapable of understanding and still less of taking action [the] natives regard all the French as wicked exploiters."[37]

While Hồ was living in Paris he formed an organization of anti-imperialists from the colonies called the Intercolonial Union. Apart from the Annamite Patriots, Syrian and Algerian activists participated. Hồ was editor of the *Paria*, the organ of the organization, which agitated for solidarity among all peoples struggling against French colonialism.[38]

---

36 Hồ Chí Minh (1962).
37 Lecountour (1968), pp. 32–33.
38 Ibid. p. 26.

Lenin's Struggle against Opportunism and Social Imperialism

During the period before and after the outbreak of WWI, Lenin was preoccupied with the link between (1) monopoly capitalism, (2) capital export, (3) imperialism, (4) colonialism, and (5) the spread of opportunism in the working class. Specifically, he struggled against the opportunist line within the Second International, which at that time played a significant role in the determination of the socialist parties' policies in Europe and North America. Should communist strategy focus on winning reforms within capitalist society, quietly moving towards a form of socialism, or could socialism ultimately only be established by an insurrectionary takeover of state power?

At the turn of the twentieth century, the center of gravity in the socialist movement had moved from England to Germany. The German working class was growing in size, strength, and political influence. Its wages grew in the years 1887–1914.[39] The German government of Chancellor Otto von Bismarck established a precursor to the postwar welfare state, with health insurance established in 1883, accident insurance in 1884, and an invalidity and old age pension in 1889. During this period the ostensibly Marxist German labor movement began a simultaneous slide from communist to reformist positions and became Europe's strongest and most influential social democractic party under the name *Sozialdemokratische Partei Deutschlands* (SPD).

---

39 Cope (2015a), p. 657.

Another Bolshevik—Grigory Zinoviev—was as preoccupied as Lenin with the role of the labor aristocracy within the socialist movement. In 1916, Zinoviev wrote "The Social Roots of Opportunism," which deals with the labor aristocracy in Germany.[40] He defined it as an upper layer of the working class, represented by the SPD apparatus. It seems that the leaders of the SPD themselves agreed. As early as 1892 Wilhelm Liebknecht, a founding member of the party (not to be confused with his son Karl Liebknecht), said at the party Congress:

> The majority of you are certainly, for the most part, aristocrats of labor, insofar as income is concerned. The working people in the mining area in Saxony and weavers in Silesia would consider incomes as yours as pure Croesus.[41]

Socialism in Western Europe was soon to lose its revolutionary élan, with the working class incorporated within the parliamentary democratic system of government. The Social Democrats became the working class's favored party. Germany's SPD, in particular, especially the "revisionist" theories of party leader Eduard Bernstein came to play an important role in the prestige enjoyed by reformism and nationalism within the socialist movement. At the general election in 1912, the party became the largest in parliament with 34.8 percent of the votes. In 1914, the German social democrats voted for war credits and Germany's participation in the War. The French and English socialists swiftly followed their lead.

---

40 Zinoviev (1942 [1916]).
41 K. Prandy et al. (1983), p. 54.

It is no wonder that the most articulate theory of imperialism and the labor aristocracy came from Europe's semi-periphery—Russia—in the form of Lenin's writings on the problematic. Lenin was forced to abandon Engels's hopes that the destruction of England's industrial monopoly would lead automatically to prerevolutionary economic conditions. On the contrary, reformism was strengthened in the socialist movement at the beginning of the 20th century. Lenin realized that this development had its roots in imperialism. The working-class leaders' "betrayal" was straightforwardly an expression of this economic relationship. Lenin describes this in his article "The International Socialist Congress in Stuttgart" in August 1907.[42] In October 1916, Lenin wrote an entire small booklet entitled *Imperialism and the Split in Socialism* specifically on the issue. It begins with the question:

> Is there any connection between imperialism and the monstrous and disgusting victory opportunism (in the form of social-chauvinism) has gained over the labor movement in Europe? *This is the fundamental question of modern socialism.* [my emphasis—TL][43]

The question of the relation between reformism and imperialism relates to the problem of nationalism versus internationalism in the labor movement. Internationalism played a central role in the early communist movement. In the *Communist Manifesto* of 1848, Marx and Engels state:

---

42 Lenin (1972 [1907]). Pages 84–86 in this book
43 Lenin (1964 [1916]), pp. 105–120. Page 133 in this book.

The working men have no country. We cannot take from them what they have not got. ... National differences and antagonisms between peoples are vanishing gradually from day to day, owing to the development of the bourgeoisie, to freedom of commerce, to the world market, to uniformity in the mode of production and in the conditions of life corresponding thereto.[44]

"Workers of the world, unite!" is the final call in the *Manifesto*. Yet it has proved to be a difficult task to achieve. The establishment and development of national states, national citizenship, and nationalist ideology played a central role in European and North American politics throughout the 1800s. This nationalism, proclaiming the national unity of all social classes, was reinforced by imperialism, with its emphasis on the white man's superiority over the "uncivilized" peoples of the colonies, as well as its international conflicts over the division of the world. The result was a broad base of at least tacit support for colonial policy in the European and North American populations.

A leading member of the British Independent Labour Party, Ramsay MacDonald, stated that a "socialist" colonial policy would have a "civilising effect" on the inhabitants of the British Empire. German Social Democrat Eduard David, meanwhile, announced that "Europe needs colonies. She does not even have enough. Without colonies, from an economic point of view, we shall sink to the level of China."[45] At the International Socialist Congress held in Stuttgart

---

44 Marx and Engels (1969 [1848]), p. 123.
45 Quoted in Clough (1992), p. 41.

in August 1907 and attended by 886 delegates from five continents—three years after German troops committed genocide in the former German colony of South West Africa, now Namibia—the chairman of the SPD, Eduard Bernstein approvingly quoted a remark made in 1863 by Ferdinand Lasalle, the party's founder: "People who cannot develop, can be justifiably subjugated by people who have achieved civilization."[46] In Germany, social democrats protested at the International Socialist Congress in Bern in 1919 against the fact that Germany was deprived of its colonies. Later, at the Labor and Socialist International Congress in Marseilles in 1925, Rudolf Hilferding demanded on behalf of German social democracy that Germany's colonies be returned to it.[47]

Lenin versus Luxemburg

Rosa Luxemburg represented the communist position in Germany. The differences between Lenin and Luxemburg were in their understanding of the role imperialism had in the colonial areas and the impact it had on the international class structure.

Lenin had previously been of the opinion that colonialism had a progressive historical role to play. The introduction and development of capitalism in the colonies, at the expense of feudal and more primitive modes of production, would create a working class and thereby prepare the ground for socialism. However, by

---

46 Wadsworth (1998), p. 99.
47 Edwards (1978), p. 39.

the outbreak of WWI Lenin held that imperialism tends toward a more permanent division of the world into nations that exploit and nations that are exploited. Capitalism had acquired a parasitic aspect during the course of its global expansion, which ensured that it would be of very limited benefit to the people of the colonial areas. Consequently, Lenin supported the movements in the colonies which fought for national independence and saw these as an important factor in the worldwide struggle for socialism.

By contrast, in vehemently opposing the rights of nations to self-determination, Luxemburg's perspective that all nationalism is bourgeois ignored the fact of some nationalisms being advanced by mainly exploited people *against* imperialist domination and others mainly by pro-imperialist, exploiting classes. Luxemburg did not discuss the inter-related concepts of superprofits, superexploitation, or superwages. She could not see imperialism's durable polarizing effect on the global class structure, or the consequences it was having for international class relations.

The imperialist solution to capitalism's problems had two sides: profitable investment opportunities in the colonies, and the expansion of an affluent market in the imperialist countries, created by a transfer of value in the form of superprofits and cheap goods to sustain superwages. While Luxemburg saw imperialism as a form of primitive accumulation, Lenin regarded imperialism as a new stage of capitalism in which the division of the world between oppressed and oppressor nations would assume paramount socio-political importance.

In Luxemburg's perspective, capitalism would spread to every corner of the globe, and thus run out of space to expand, and the resulting underconsumption crisis (wherein capitalists are unable to sell their surplus commodities to pre-capitalist markets) would lead inexorably to systemic collapse. This crisis would be followed by a socialist revolution led by the working class in the imperialist countries, who would then hand over independence to the colonies.[48] As such, Luxemburg regarded the emerging anti-colonial nationalism as basically bourgeois.[49] The working class in the colonial areas was not developed enough to take the leadership of the national movements. Therefore, for Luxemburg, as for Trotsky, the working class in the developed imperialist countries was the driving force in socialist world revolution.

The appeal by Luxemburg for Europe's workers not to go to war against each other was, however, in vain. Under the leadership of the Social Democratic parties, the workers followed their respective national bourgeoisies into the first inter-imperialist war for colonies and spheres of influence. The interests of the bourgeoisie and the upper layers of the working class fused with a drive to common national prosperity. Lenin noted in May 1915 that the Second International had to collapse because of nationalism and opportunism in the imperialist country working class.[50]

Luxemburg's strategy came to a fatal end with the abortive German revolution of 1919, when the social democrats chose to side with the bourgeoisie against the communist revolutionaries. Even with the political impetus of the workers' movement as measured by

---

48 Rosa Luxemburg (1951), pp. 365–369.
49 Kerswell (2011), p. 119.
50 Lenin (1974 [1915]). Pages 93–96 in this book

Table I. Results of the German Federal Election of January 19, 1919[51]

Name of Party and Core Constituency	No. of Seats
Independent Socialists [Revolutionary and/or Anti-War Left]	23
Majority Socialists (Social-Democrats) [Organized Working Class and Labor Aristocracy]	163
Democratic Party [Bourgeois Liberal]	75
Centre [Catholic]	91
German National People's Party (former National Liberals) [Big Industrialists]	22
Nationalist (former Conservatives) [Agrarian elites, Army Officers, Monarchists]	42
Minor Parties	10

its authority and the strength of the workers' and soldiers' councils formed in 1918, the results of the first free Parliamentary elections that Germany had ever seen show clearly that the vast majority of Germans—even after four years of fighting an atrocious imperialist war—were opposed to implementing socialism (see Table I). Rather, around 82 percent of the German electorate desired a liberal-democratic Republic. The SPD itself early on assisted in removing "every obstacle to the domination of the great industrialists, who proceeded to reorganize the economic life of the country on the

51 Ibid., p. 155.

basis of mixed or vertical trusts."[52]

Tragically, Luxemburg and her comrade Karl Liebknecht were murdered in the process of the postwar consolidation of German capitalism. The following decades came to show the extent to which it was possible for German imperialism to mobilize the working class in an attempt to reinstate Germany's leading position in the imperialist world order.

The Formation of the Comintern and the Colonial Question

Lenin struggled against social chauvinism (that is, the national chauvinism of titular socialists) in his political practice and in his many articles on the subject. One of the arenas of struggle was the international communist movement. The Second International collapsed formally in 1917, but in reality it had already done so at the outbreak of WWI. Its replacement, the Comintern was created in 1919 with Lenin's Bolsheviks, now in power in the Soviet Union, as the driving force. At this point, the Comintern still considered that it was in Europe that the main battle for the world revolution had to occur. The supposition was that the revolutionary line would prevail over the nationalist and reformist social democratic line. Lenin emphasized repeatedly that an understanding of the roots of opportunism and the fight against social-chauvinism was

---

52 Smith (1942), p. 157.

the main task of Western European revolutionaries in this period.[53]
His political strategy for Western Europe at the end of WWI was
to bypass the upper, highest paid layers of the working class and to
organize and mobilize the proletariat proper for the revolution. This
strategy was applied not least in Germany, which had lost the war,
been stripped of its colonies, and been fleeced by the other imperialist powers' demands for war reparations. Lenin saw the revolution
in Germany as essential for the survival of the Russian revolution
and for the further advance of the world revolution. In a political
report to the Central Committee on March 7, 1918, Lenin wrote:

> History has now placed us in an extraordinarily difficult posi-
> tion; in the midst of organisational work of unparalleled diffi-
> culty we shall have to experience a number of painful defeats.
> Regarded from the world-historical point of view, there would
> doubtlessly be no hope of the ultimate victory of our revolu-
> tion if it were to remain alone, if there were no revolutionary
> movements in other countries….. I repeat, our salvation from
> all these difficulties is an all Europe revolution.[54]

However, as noted above, the German revolution did not transpire,
and this placed the future of the world revolution in jeopardy.

---

53 Lenin (1972a [1917]). Pages 159–160 in this book.
54 Lenin (1972b [1918]).

The Second Comintern Congress:
West or East?

Concerning solidarity with the colonized people, not much was gained from the European Social Democrats. Lenin spoke of the treason of the British working class toward the oppressed nations' struggle for freedom at the Communist International's Second Congress in July 1920.[55] Indeed, the British Labour Party program of 1918 made it clear that the party was against the disestablishment of the British Empire, since it considered it its duty to "defend the rights of British citizens who have overseas interests." It went so far as to declare of Britain's Empire of plunder: "As for this community of races and peoples of different colours, religions and different stages of civilization, which is called the British Empire, the Labour Party is in favor of its maintenance."[56]

In the case of India, the British Labour Party formally supported independence, but continually stalled the process leading up to it, including by cracking down on massive nationalist dissent with recourse to military force. British Marxist Rajani Palme Dutt cited an article from the *Manchester Guardian* of 1930 by way of explanation for Britain's continual intransigence vis-à-vis Indian nationalism. It said: "There are two chief reasons why a self-regarding England may hesitate to relax her control over India. The first is that her influence in the past depends partly upon her power to summon troops and to draw resources from India in time of need

---

55 Lenin (1965b [1920]). Pages 180–186 in this book.
56 Edwards (1978), p. 39.

... The second is that Great Britain finds in India her best market, and she has £1,000 million of capital invested there."[57]

Little wonder, then, that communists from the colonies began to attack Eurocentrism in the communist movement. Pak Din Shoon, the Korean delegate at the Congress, criticized the way the colonial question was treated in the first Congress, stating: "The attention should have been directed to the East, where the fate of the world revolution may very well be decided."[58] Meanwhile, the Indian delegate Manabendra Nath Roy, Head of the Comintern's Far Eastern Bureau, placed the exploitation of the colonies centrally in the discussion of international communist strategy:

> Superprofits gained in the colonies are the mainstay of modern capitalism, and as long as these exist, it will be difficult for the European working class to overthrow the capitalist order ... By exploiting the masses in the colonies, European imperialism is in a position to make concession after concession to the labor aristocracy at home.[59]

Another interesting figure in the same debate was Mirsaid Sultan Galiev, who came from the Muslim part of the old Russian Empire, and had participated in the revolution of 1917. Galiev also recommended that the Comintern give priority to anti-colonial revolutions in the East, with the correct argument that losing the underdeveloped world to exploit is a precondition for revolution in the West:

---

57 Dutt (1940), p. 497; cf. Cope (2008), p. 256.
58 Quoted in Bashear (1980), p. 13.
59 Ibid., p. 14.

"Deprived of the East, and cut off from India, Afghanistan, Persia, and its other Asian and African colonies, Western European imperialism will wither and die a natural death."[60] Galiev thought that the communist movement had made a serious strategic error by "giving first priority to the revolutionary movement in Western Europe, and thus had overlooked the fact that capitalism's weak point lay in the Orient."[61] For Galiev, who was implacably opposed to any and all industrial society, and not simply the capitalist variety, the East may not have had a developed working class, but the nations therein were exploited and therefore "proletarian nations."[62] A similar point to Galiev's had been made by Li Dazhao, one of the founders of Marxism in China. In January 1920 he described China as "proletarianized in relation to the world system."[63]

The Baku Conference

Both before and after its disagreements with the "national communism" of the Caucasus (and of the Ukraine), the Comintern prioritized the issue of the Far East and the Muslim population in and around the new Soviet State.

Toward that end, on September 1, 1920, the Comintern organized the First Congress of the Peoples of the East in Baku, Azerbaijan.

---

60 Sultan-Galiev (1979 [1919]), p. 136.
61 Bennigsen (1958), p. 404.
62 Roberts (1990), p. 39
63 Meisner (1970), p. 401.

With around 1,900 delegates, the Congress was a mixed gathering of communists, anarchists, and radical nationalists. The Baku Congress was one of the first forums where anti-colonial activists met to discuss ideas and exchange opinions on the future of the "peoples of the East" after the War. The ambition of the congress was to establish a common understanding amongst the delegates on "the fight against imperialist domination and capitalist exploitation."[64] A far-reaching objective was to form an alliance between the Comintern and the colonial liberation movements in Asia and "to win them fully to communism."

Grigori Zinoviev, the Chairman of the Comintern, promised at the Congress that the Comintern intended to support the liberation movements in Turkey, Persia, and the Transcaucasian Republics. The gathering adopted a formal "Manifesto of the Peoples of the East" as well as an "Appeal to the Workers of Europe, America, and Japan," exhorting them to support the anti-imperialist struggle. An executive body was elected to carry on the Comintern's work in the Middle East and Far East. Moscow also allotted 750,000 gold rubles—at a time when the country appeared close to bankruptcy and faced serious famine—to extend the ranges of two radio stations from 12,000 to 20,000 kilometers, making them probably the most powerful in the world. One of them was to be situated at Nicolaev in Central Siberia to broadcast anti-imperialist propaganda to the colonized nations of Asia.[65]

---

64 Rustamova-Tohidi (1996); Weiner (1996), p. 162; cf. Petersson (2013), p. 57.
65 Cave Brown and Macdonald (1981), p. 189.

In the Far East the national liberation movement had assumed extraordinary proportions in connection with the Chinese nationalist struggle against Japanese imperialism. For the Comintern, this movement represented a vital basis upon which to establish support for its anti-imperialist policy, especially after the revolutionary tide in Europe had petered out at the beginning of the 1920s. In March 1925, the chairperson of the Comintern, Nikolai Bukharin, concluded that the colonial question was "nothing but the question of the relations between town and country on a world scale."[66] This formulation was to be echoed decades later by Aidat, a leading theorist in the Indonesian Communist Party:

> On a world scale, Asia, Africa, and Latin America are the village of the world, while Europe and North America is the town of the world. If the world revolution is to be victorious, there is no other way than for the world proletariat to give prominence to the revolutions in Asia, Africa, and Latin America, that is to say, the revolutions in the village of the world. In order to win the world revolution the world proletariat must go to these three continents.[67]

It was also the main thesis of the Vice Premier of the People's Republic of China, Marshall Lin Biao, as expounded in his *Long Live the Victory of Peoples War!* written in 1965. As the Chinese Revolution revolved around the rural areas surrounding and taking over the urban areas in a protracted people's war, Lin advocated

---

66 Bukharin (1956 [1925]), p. 201.
67 Aidat (1964), cited in Johnson (1973), p. 64.

the application of this strategy on a world scale, with the Third
World countries cast as the global countryside and the First World
the global city.

The Fifth Comintern Congress
and the League against Imperialism (LAI)

In late 1923, Hồ left Paris and arrived in Moscow to begin work
for the Comintern. Lenin died shortly before Hồ arrived, but nev-
ertheless he met with leading Bolsheviks such as Bukharin, Karl
Radek, Leon Trotsky, and Josef Stalin. Hồ participated in the 5th
Congress of the Comintern of June/July 1924, where he criticized the
French Communist Party (PCF) for ignoring the colonial question.[68]

> You must excuse my frankness, but I cannot help but observe
> that the speeches by comrades from the mother countries give
> me the impression that they wish to kill a snake by stepping
> on its tail. You all know today the poison and life energy of
> the capitalist snake is concentrated more in the colonies than
> in the mother countries. ... Yet in our discussion of the rev-
> olution you neglect to talk about the colonies ... Why do you
> neglect the colonies, while capitalism uses them to support
> itself, defend itself, and fight you?[69]

---

68 Lacouture (1968), p. 41.
69 Nguyen Ai Quoc (1974 [1924]), p. 809.

Hồ issued a sharp criticism of all the European communist parties for their lack of solidarity with the proletariat of the colonies:

> Thus, it is not an exaggeration to say that so long as the French and British Communist Parties have not brought out a really progressive policy with regard to the colonies and have not come into contact with the colonial peoples, their programme as a whole is and will be ineffective because it goes counter to Leninism.
>
> According to Lenin, the victory of the revolution in Western Europe depended on its close contact with the liberation movement against imperialism in enslaved colonies and with the national question, both of which form a part of the common problem of the proletarian revolution and dictatorship.
>
> As for our Communist Parties in Great Britain, Holland, Belgium and other countries—what have they done to cope with the colonial invasions perpetrated by the bourgeois class of their countries? What have they done from the day they accepted Lenin's political programme to educate the working class of their countries in the spirit of just internationalism, and that of close contact with the working masses in the colonies? What our Parties have done in this domain is almost worthless. As for me, I was born in a French colony, and am a member of the French Communist Party, and I am very sorry to say that our Communist Party has done hardly anything for the colonies.[70]

---

70 Hồ Chí Minh (1960 [1924]).

Hồ Chí Minh's criticism was never understood, much less acted upon by the communist parties of the imperialist countries, however, which persisted in their lukewarm approach to the colonial question. Worse still, the social democratic parties, at the time representing the majority of the working class in Western European countries, proved to be directly *pro*-imperialist. In 1925, Hồ left for Canton in China, where he developed contacts within the Chinese Communist Party. He also visited Siam (Thailand) and other Asian countries to coordinate Comintern activities.

In the mid-1920s, the Comintern worked together with German communist Willi Münzenberg to establish a more broad-based organization to develop the struggle against imperialism. The task of the League against Imperialism (LAI) was to coordinate and develop the anti-imperialist struggle in both the colonies and in the imperialist countries, as well as between them. That is to say, the LAI aimed to make the shift from anti-colonialism to anti-imperialism, and to place the Comintern in a central position in this struggle.

The LAI headquarters was in Berlin. As noted, Germany had lost its colonies through defeat in WWI and the German state power was therefore less repressive towards anti-colonial movements. After years of preparation, the LAI was launched at a conference in Brussels in February 1927. A total of 174 delegates representing 134 organizations from 34 countries attended the Congress.[71] Albert Einstein—nominated as Honorary President of the LAI at the end of the Congress—stated: "In your congress, the solidly united endeavor of the oppressed to achieve independence takes

---

71 Petersson (2013), p. 136.

bodily shape."[72] Jawaharlal Nehru (who became the first Prime Minister of India in 1947) also attended the Brussels Congress and was elected to the LAI Executive Committee. He participated in the session "British Imperialism in India, Persia and Mesopotamia," along with the Persian Ahmed Assadoff (who lived in Berlin), and met with other delegates from Java, Indo-China, Palestine, Syria, Egypt, North Africa, and Sub-Saharan Africa. Nehru was greatly impressed by the moral courage displayed by "quite a number of distinguished persons" the organizers had invited, or who had themselves become aware of the Congress, luminaries such as Einstein, Soong Qingling (Madame Sun Yat Sen), and Nobel Laureate Romain Rolland.[73]

Another participant who would become at least as well-known was Hồ Chí Minh, at that time an experienced Comintern emissary. He met and conferred with other anti-colonial activists, for example, Sukarno (the First President of Indonesia following independence from the Netherlands), Soong Qingling, and leading Japanese Socialist and later Prime Minister Tetsu Katayama.[74] The LAI Congress was the first time so many activists from so many colonies had met to exchange experiences and coordinate their struggles. It was in that sense of profound historic importance. When the Indonesian President Sukarno gave the opening speech at the first Afro-Asian Conference held in Bandung in 1955, he referred to the LAI Conference in 1927 as an important reference point of

---

72 Ibid., p. 137.
73 Nehru (1953 [1936]), p. 139.
74 Duiker (2000), pp. 148–9; cf. Petersson (2013), p. 205.

the anti-colonial struggle.

Besides its headquarters in Berlin, the LAI established national secretariats in Paris, London, Amsterdam, and Boston, which were to advance anti-imperialist work together with the national communist parties. Unfortunately, however, this part of the work never left the ground. The European communist parties were not especially enthusiastic about anti-imperialism. They knew very well that it was not a burning issue for the European working class, and was very often considered unpatriotic. Thus, in spite of repeated and unsparing criticism from the Comintern, the European national communist parties never prioritized the anti-imperialist struggle. In addition to the relative indifference of the European communists, the LAI was under constant pressure and harassment from the various European intelligence agencies.

As such, the LAI never became the instrument Münzerberg and the Comintern had intended it to be. In 1933, when the National Socialist Party came to power in Germany, the LAI had to move to Paris, and when Germany occupied France the LAI ceased to exist. Münzenberg was interned by the French authorities in southern France. He managed to escape, but soon disappeared, and his fate remains unknown. Hồ Chí Minh's statement about the difficult task of mobilizing the European working class for anti-imperialism turned out to be all too correct. In the colonies, however, the national liberation struggle gained ground, and in that respect the LAI was not without an impact. The LAI certainly contributed to the fact that the national liberation struggles embraced Marxism-Leninism and communists became leading figures in the freedom struggle in the colonies.

The Sixth Comintern Congress

The plenum at the 6th Congress of the Comintern, held in Moscow in July–August 1928, agreed on the necessity to reorganize the Eastern Department in order to make anti-colonial work operational. Thus, the overarching aim was to get the Eastern Department to establish an organization, supported by "propaganda sub-departments," under the leadership of twenty-four "comrades from eight Eastern countries." The primary aim of this re-organization was to confirm contact with non-communist revolutionary organizations and help them to work out their programme and tactics.[75]

At the Congress, Otto Kuusinen[76] presented a document entitled "Theses on the Revolutionary Movement in Colonial and Semi-Colonial Countries," which once again criticized the communist parties' weak anti-imperialist efforts:

> It must be admitted that, up till now, not all the parties in the Communist International have fully grasped the decisive importance which the establishment of close, regular and unbroken relations with the national revolutionary movements in the colonies has in affording these movements active and practical help.[77]

---

75 Degras (1960), p. 247.
76 Otto W. Kuusinen (1881–1964) was a Finnish and, later, Soviet communist and literary historian. After the defeat of the Reds in the Finnish Civil War, he fled to the Soviet Union where he worked until his death.
77 "Theses on the Revolutionary Movement in Colonial and Semi-Colonial Countries," adopted by the 6th Comintern Congress, 1928, in Degras (1960), pp. 526–548.

In his presentation of the colonial "theses," Kuusinen stated that the communist parties' colonial work was "one of the weakest sides of Comintern activity." From the formation of the Comintern in 1919 up until 1928, the communist parties had either chosen to ignore their colonial work completely or considered it a complete waste of time.[78] The Comintern headquarters struggled against this trend and tried to set a course for anti-colonial work in the Communist Parties and the LAI in Western Europe. Kuusinen endorsed a small Commission headed by British Communist Robin Page Arnot to visit the Western European parties in order to gather intelligence on their colonial work and prepare for yet another "Colonial Conference" in the spring of 1929.[79]

In London, the Communist Party of Great Britain (CPGB) had huge problems in adjusting itself to the line of the Comintern on anti-colonial policy. Arnot attended the CPGB congress and observed how the party discussed the colonial question. Arnot reported to Kuusinen in January 1929 that, apparently, "on the last day" some delegates raised the question in a passing fashion, forcing Arnot to concede that the CPGB's capacity to carry out colonial work was in a poor state.[80]

---

78 Ibid., pp. 526, 537–547; cf. Petersson (2013), p. 253.

79 Robin Page Arnot (1890–1986) was a founding member of the CPGB in 1920. He was imprisoned for being a conscientious objector during WWI, and imprisoned again in 1925 before the General Strike. He was a Central Committee member and CPGB Comintern contact.

80 According to Arnot, the CPGB should continue to carry out the "task of ideological strengthening of the Party," a process that "will … take some time and much vigilance to weed out the right wing tendencies."

Arnot's next stop was Paris. Arnot realized that the state of the colonial work in the PCF was, if anything, even worse than its British counterpart. Arnot could confirm the experiences of Nguyên Ai Quôc during his work for the PCF. The party had an indolent attitude towards its colonial work, as William Duiker writes in his biography of Hô Chí Minh, existing only "on paper" and not in reality.[81] Arnot summed up his impressions in "Report on the Parties," which was a ruthless criticism of the incompetence of the communist parties. According to this report, the parties in France, Great Britain, Belgium, and the Netherlands shared the stigma of not being able to carry out the simplest of tasks, for instance finding colonial contacts, and lamented that "at the moment not much is being done."[82]

An observation which corresponds with Matthew Worley's conclusion that the CPGB was around this time "plagued by internal conflict and ... political stupefaction." Handwritten letter from R. Page Arnot to Otto Kuusinen in Moscow, January 29, 1929, cited in Worley (2002), p. 116; cf. Petersson (2013), p. 257.
81 Duiker (2000), pp. 148–150.
82 Russian State Archive for Social and Political History. 495/154/364, 52–54, Report on the Parties, Arnot, February 1929, cited in Petersson (2013), p. 258.

The Colonial Conference of 1929 and the "Magyar Thesis"

After receiving Arnot's report the commission that prepared the Colonial Conference concluded that it was essential to formulate a new thesis on colonial work. The task was given to Ludwig Magyar, who wrote "The Organisation of the Colonial Work of the European Communist Parties."[83] Magyar argued that the ignorance and apparent failure of the communist parties in Europe to conduct any kind of colonial work deserved unsparing criticism. He concluded:

> The most important tasks of the Communist Parties of the imperialist countries with regard to the colonial question is: first the establishment of a direct contact between the Communist Parties and the revolutionary trade union organisations ... The relationships existing up to now between the Communist Parties and the revolutionary movement in the respective colonial countries cannot be considered ... as satisfactory. ... Not all of the Parties of the CI [Comintern] have so far

---

83 Russian State Archive for Social and Political History 495/18/670, 49–55. Confidential resolution: The Organisation of the Colonial Work of the European Communist Parties, author: Ludwig Magyar. Moscow, 29/3–1929 in Petersson (2013), pp. 264–65. Ludwig Magyar (1891–1937), real name Layos Milgrof, was a Hungarian communist and journalist. After the fall of the Hungarian Soviet republic in 1919 he was arrested, but in 1922 he benefited from an exchange of prisoners between Hungary and Russia. He then settled in Moscow where he worked for the Comintern. He was executed in 1937 on charges relating to the assassination of Leningrad Party leader Sergei Kirov.

grasped the great significance of regular close connections with the revolutionary movements in the colonies for the active immediate practical support of these movements. Only to the extent that the Communist Parties in the imperialist countries actually support the revolutionary movement [and] assist the struggle of [the] colonial countries against imperialism, can their position with regard to the colonial question be accepted as truly Bolshevik. This is the criterion for their revolutionary activity in general.

Magyar had distinguished five fields of activity which the parties had to implement in their colonial work, the first two being to organize a system to distribute political literature from Europe to the colonies and to ensure that correspondence from Europe arrived in the hands of revolutionary organizations and individuals in the colonies. In addition, members of European communist parties should accept their duty to travel to the colonies, acting as "emigrants" and not as "representatives" or "emissaries" of the Comintern. Once on location, the "emigrants" should blend in with the everyday life of the workers and carry out manual labor in order to establish contacts with political activists at the grassroots level. The fourth field of activity focused on getting the parties to establish contacts with sailors, workers, soldiers, and students from colonial countries living in the "big cities of the capitalist countries." Once contact was an established fact, the communists then had to "penetrate into the ranks" of the colonial communities in the metropolitan cities with the sole purpose of exerting "Communist influence … among them." Magyar's final point focused on the failure of the central committees of the communist parties to organise "routine colonial work," a crucial question for the Comintern which the parties were urged to cease ignoring.[84]

What is entirely missing from Magyar's recommendations, however, was how to struggle against imperialist policies in the European and North American nations themselves, and how to mobilize the working classes there against imperialist wars and racism.

From Anti-Imperialism to Anti-Fascism

Lenin's and the Comintern's many attempts to implement anti-imperialism in the policy of the Communist parties in the West were thwarted. The European attitude towards the colonies, both in the general population and far into the ranks of the socialists, was that they should serve the "mother country" and its needs. It was almost seen by many as the moral and political duty of the advanced capitalist countries to benefit from and properly utilise the wealth and resources of Asia, Africa, and Latin America, since the colonies would supposedly thereby become developed and civilized. The human cost involved and the distortion of the colonised country's economy was at best considered an unfortunate byproduct of this "civilising mission," a sort of world historical "collateral damage." The Communist parties were aware of this chauvinistic attitude, and thought it futile to go against it. There is, in fact, little doubt that a strong anti-imperialist profile would have made it

---

84 Petersson (2013), p. 265.

difficult to attract members and mobilize for the European class struggle nationally.

Appraising the policy of Lenin and the Comintern during this period, Fritz Sternberg wrote in 1935:

> As Lenin misjudged the real strength of Reformism so did his epigones even more. He never gave a systematic analysis of the sociological prerequisites which formed the basis of Reformism, and which prevented it from being shaken during the period up to the victory of Fascism. The Comintern has contented itself with slogans. It has never made it clear that the differentiation in the pre-war years within the working class took place based on the increasing wages of the entire class.
>
> The Comintern has not corrected Lenin's mistake as to the question of the labor aristocracy and thus the evaluation of the real strength of Reformism. On the contrary: it has made it even deeper.[85]

Sternberg was proved correct insofar as the German working class developed a particularly unpleasant kind of labor aristocracy during the Nazi period. Earlier, when the leaders of the SPD gathered after Adolf Hitler's appointment as Chancellor by President Paul von Hindenburg on January 30, 1933, they concluded that the time had not yet arrived for mass protest and, instead, "endorsed

---

85 Sternberg (1935), p. 91. Friedrich "Fritz" Sternberg (1895–1963) was a German economist, historian, and social democratic politician. He was much influenced by Rosa Luxemburg's understanding of imperialism.

passivity."[86] On May 17 that same year, Chancellor Hitler announced that he would make a statement in the Reichstag assuring Europe of Germany's commitment to peace. The SPD debated whether to attend this session, whether or not to endorse Hitler's resolution, and whether or not to make a formal protest over the incarceration of hundreds of social democrats and the mass repression being conducted against the party. In the end, 48 out of 65 SPD deputies voted to endorse Hitler's declaration and almost every SPD deputy (aside from Carlo Mierendorff, Kurt Schumacher and, also, Toni Pfülf, who tragically committed suicide shortly after, indicating her profound sense that social democratic principles had been betrayed) attended the Reichstag session:

> When the Social Democratic deputies rose as a body to vote with the bourgeois parties the chamber, including Hitler, broke into a storm of applause. The German Nationalists burst into *Deutschland, Deutschland, über Alles*, and many Social Democrats joined in. [Bavarian parliamentarian Wilhelm] Hoegner later reflected, "It was as if we Social Democrats, ever cursed as the prodigal sons of the fatherland, for one eternal moment clasped Mother Germany to our hearts."[87]

By 1937, the SPD in exile were forced to concede that the Nazi form of the social imperialism they themselves had earlier pursued by peaceful means was yielding political capital for the regime. "The experience of recent years," said the newspaper of the émigré SPD,

---

86 Harsch (1993), p. 225.
87 Ibid., p. 236.

the *Deutschland-Berichte (Sopade)*, "has unfortunately demonstrated that the petit-bourgeois inclinations of part of the working class are unfortunately greater than we had earlier recognized."[88] Burleigh and Wippermann characterize this as being "in the nature of an understatement."[89]

Until 1934, the Comintern had attacked the Social Democrats' pro-imperialism, but in light of the rise of fascism the Comintern changed its line in the mid-1930s to a "popular front" strategy that once more sought cooperation with Social Democracy. Thus in Dimitrov's report for the 7th Congress of the Comintern in 1935, he only mentioned the struggle in the colonies almost in passing. Rather, the defeat of fascism in Europe was the main objective. In this fight, he listed a number of progressive forces: Social Democrats, Catholics, anarchists, unorganized workers, peasants, the petty bourgeoisie, and the intelligentsia. At the end of this list the peoples' struggle in the colonies are mentioned as an "important reserve for the world proletariat."[90]

To be sure, there was a rationale in this tactical alliance, namely, to prevent German imperialism from starting a new war against the Soviet Union. There is no doubt, in fact, that a Nazi victory would have immeasurably galvanized the forces of world imperialism. However, positing a strict dividing line between fascist and "democratic" states inevitably sidetracked the anti-colonial struggle, which became a positive problem where it obstructed the "Allies"

---

88 Burleigh and Wippermann (2011 [1991]), p. 294.
89 Ibid.
90 Dimitrov (1973 [1935]), p. 59.

in the fight against fascism. Thus whereas the Communist Party of India attracted mass support following the Bengal famine of 1943— caused by British overexploitation of the country to finance the war effort, an attendant "war boom," and rapid inflation—it had taken a resolutely anti-nationalist position following the German invasion of the USSR in 1941.

Revolutionary socialism died out in Europe and never got a foothold in North America, instead gaining its strength in the Global East and South. It is noteworthy that virtually all revolutionary attempts in the last hundred years have occurred either in the world periphery, or in the semi-periphery of the imperialist centre (in the second place, not only in Russia, but less successfully with the struggles of the New Afrikan, American Indian, and Chicano/a people in the U.S., the Basque people, and the Irish for national liberation). The Russian Revolution signaled a decisive shift in the centre of gravity of the communist movement, from Europe to the periphery. This change came to shape the history of revolution in the twentieth century. In China the Taiping Revolution of 1911 preceded a continuous wave of revolutionary struggle up until the establishment of the People's Republic in 1949. In Mexico, there was a revolutionary upsurge between 1910 and 1930. After WWII the wave of anti-colonial revolutions resumed and the 1960s and 1970s witnessed revolutionary uprisings in Asia, Africa, and Latin America.

The Parasite State and its Class Struggles

When the CWC in the late 1960s encountered the lack of revolutionary spirit and the absence of solidarity with the freedom struggle in Vietnam, there was much inspiration to be drawn from Lenin's struggle against opportunism, and he provided an answer to the question about the reason for this situation: imperialism and the rise of the "parasite state."

Today there is a world of difference between political struggles in the Global South and Global North, though each is part of the same capitalist world system. The economic base is different, as is the political framework of the state. Unquestionably, the parasite state in the Global North is capitalist and its logic is driven by the goal of protecting investments and securing markets. The private ownership of the means of production is guaranteed by the Constitution and the institutions of state. However, a distinct form of the capitalist state is in place. The system of government is parliamentary democracy with universal suffrage, with the state upholding the rule of law and at least pretending to guarantee freedom of organization and of expression. Such a state formation can hardly be described as being in the hands of a bourgeoisie wielding untrammeled and unconcealed class power. Who, then, has the power in the parasite state and what is the nature of the class struggle therein?

The relatively peaceful form that class struggle takes in the North does not mean that the state is an expression of cooperation and reconciliation, or that class struggle has ended there. The emergence and development of the state are the result of class conflict in society, yet as Engels writes:

51

> [In] order that these antagonisms, classes with conflicting economic interests, shall not consume themselves and society in fruitless struggle, a power, apparently standing above society, has become necessary to moderate the conflict and keep it within the bounds of "order"; and this power, arisen out of society, but placing itself above it and increasingly alienating itself from it, is the state.[91]

A specific example of the relative class autonomy of the state, beginning around 1850, is the factory inspections. The inspectors' task was to ensure that the state's rules on working conditions in the factories were observed by the capitalists. These rules and regulations on the length of the working day, child labor, and so forth were not enforced by the power of the working class, which was at the time still weak and disorganized. The bourgeoisie was adamantly opposed to the efforts to reduce the working day and thus its profits. It was the state—personified by the factory inspectors—that carried out this scrutiny, intended to save the working class from being consumed by the greed of individual capitalists, so that the capitalist mode of production as a whole might be maintained.

The state is a social relation, with "the exercise of state power (or, better, state powers in the plural) [being] a form-determined condensation of the changing balance of class forces."[92] Just as the absolutist state in the 17th century represented a sharing of power between the feudal nobility and the ascendant bourgeoisie, the

---

91 Engels (2010 [1884]), chapter IX, "Barbarism and Civilization."
92 Jessop (2002), p. 40; cf. Poulantzas (1978).

modern liberal parliamentary state represents a division of power between capital and large sections of the working class. From a Marxist point of view, there is nothing new or controversial in a conception of state power that emphasizes its relative independence from the bourgeoisie, nor in suggesting that the state may represent a sharing of power between classes within the overall framework of capitalism. Marx himself gives a concrete example of a government that reflects a sharing of power between the bourgeoisie and the working class in his writings on the civil war in France:

> The empire, with the coup d'etat for its birth certificate, universal suffrage for its sanction, and the sword for its sceptre, professed to rest upon the peasantry, the large mass of producers not directly involved in the struggle of capital and labor. It professed to save the working class by breaking down parliamentarism, and, with it, the undisguised subserviency of government to the propertied classes. It professed to save the propertied classes by upholding their economic supremacy over the working class; and, finally, it professed to unite all classes by reviving for all the chimera of national glory.
>
> In reality, it was the only form of government possible at a time when the bourgeoisie had already lost, and the working class had not yet acquired, the faculty of ruling the nation. It was acclaimed throughout the world as the savior of society. Under its sway, bourgeois society, freed from political cares, attained a development unexpected even by itself.[93]

---

93 Marx (1959 [1871]), p. 150.

Lenin gave the following famous description of parliamentary democracy:

> A democratic republic is the best possible political shell for capitalism, and, therefore, once capital has gained possession of this very best shell, it establishes its power so securely, so firmly, that no change of persons, institutions or parties in the bourgeois-democratic republic can shake it.[94]

Marx had already described how this bourgeois republican constitution works. It is a constitution that by universal suffrage gives political power to the classes whose subordination it guarantees. The constitution thus deprives the bourgeoisie of political hegemony so that it can maintain the social power that same Constitution authorizes:

> The comprehensive contradiction of this constitution, however, consists in the following: The classes whose social slavery the constitution is to perpetuate—proletariat, peasantry, petty bourgeoisie—it puts in possession of political power through universal suffrage. And from the class whose old social power it sanctions, the bourgeoisie, it withdraws the political guarantees of this power. It forces the political rule of the bourgeoisie into democratic conditions, which at every moment help the hostile classes to victory and jeopardize the very foundations of bourgeois society. From the first group it demands that they should not go forward from political to

---

94 Lenin (1964a [1917]), chapter III, "The State: an Instrument for the Exploitation of the Oppressed Class."

social emancipation; from the others that they should not go back from social to political restoration.[95]

Contemporary European constitutions function in a similar way. In the liberal parliamentary system, the executive power does not represent the exclusive interests either of capital or of the working class, but simply the prevailing mode of production, with state power accruing to the class or classes best placed to maintain and expand it. The private ownership of the means of production—and with it bourgeois economic domination—is guaranteed by the law. However, through universal suffrage, the constitution also necessitates the bourgeoisie taking political account of the lower classes. Thus, the constitution requires that the working class not use its political freedom (universal suffrage, freedom of expression and organization) to pursue its economic freedom. On the other hand, the bourgeoisie must content itself with economic power, and not demand exclusive political preeminence.[96]

---

95 Marx (2000 [1850]), p. 319.
96 At a particular conjuncture, however, the alignment of class forces can change, and with it the form taken by the political domination of the bourgeoisie. Nicos Poulantzas has argued that fascism got its central impetus from monopoly capital's need to remove the major political obstacles to its expansion. In Germany, monopoly capital was restricted by the parliamentary system and by the anachronistic antagonisms within this system between fractions of capital, and between capital as a whole and the organized working class. Fascism offered monopoly capital both a means to unify and consolidate bourgeois hegemony over the nation and to forcefully inure itself against a socialist backlash. Fascist management of the capitalist economy was intended to regulate it in the interests of

The reason why the working class struggle is limited to the framework of capitalism is, of course, imperialism and the establishment of the parasitic state. The economistic trend in the working class movement, that is, the confinement of its tasks to struggles for higher wages and better working conditions, was already apparent to Marx and Engels and had become even more so to Lenin, who fought against the social and political *embourgeoisement* that underpinned it. It was only after WWII, however, that it became clear that Lenin's description of a labor aristocracy had begun to cover the great majority of the First World working class.

Today, the labor aristocracy is not merely a thin upper stratum of workers in any given country, nor is social chauvinism a passing trend (as the term "opportunism" may falsely imply). The contradiction "bourgeoisie–working class" in the imperialist countries is no longer the dominant factor in the two classes' respective development. The contradiction between them is primarily influenced by the fact that they stand united in another, more primary contradiction,

---

one or more monopolistic combines and to attack the organized forms of the proletariat whilst managing state resources to provide for those sectors whose labor was not required for imperialist growth, namely, the petty bourgeoisie. During the economic crisis of the 1920s, the German petty bourgeoisie found its material privileges compromised. Some of its members turned towards the reformist capitalism of the Social Democratic Party (SPD). Still others, tired of the inertia of the SPD's ever more precarious balancing act between the working class and big business, turned towards fascism. The German petty bourgeoisie was used to a high standard of living and in anti-proletarian dread of losing it. Fascism answered the needs of the petty bourgeoisie and ascendant sections of the working class in seemingly terminal crisis.

namely, that between the exploiting nations and the exploited nations.

For the most part, repression has faded into the background for the majority therein. Instead, the imperialist state seeks to unite the people and government in a mutually reinforcing symbiotic relation to the nation. Only national citizens are entitled to receive benefits from the state; non-citizens are excluded. Imperialism creates a mutual sense and an institutional structure of common national interest between the state and its citizens. It is this that Dr. M.G.E. Kelly calls "biopolitical imperialism":

> I will argue that biopolitics constitutes a missing link in explaining how imperialism involves the ordinary people of the First World. For one thing, biopolitics provides a mechanism by which the profits of imperialism may be spread to a whole population. By uniting us in a single population, moreover, biopolitics generates solidarity between ordinary people and elites.[97]

Imperialist parasitism is not only reflected in superprofits for capital, then, or in the cheap popular consumption afforded by the matrix of superexploitation, but also in the way that state power manages the population. In real terms, the social benefits afforded the poorest people in the Global North is at least ten times greater than the income of the average Indian. The biological indicators follow the same pattern, with an average north European living 16 years longer than the average Indian.[98] The capitalist welfare state grew as a new means for the imperialist state to influence its population.

---

97 Kelly (2015), p. 19.
98 World Health Organisation (2014), p. 7.

The Welfare State

The First World state is committed to a welfare system with public health, education, social security, and pensions. There are certainly differences in the extent and composition of social expenditure between different states in the North, but most liberal and conservative politicians remain committed to the general welfare even under neoliberalism. Indeed, between 1980 and 2014, average social expenditure in the OECD countries increased from 15.4 percent of GDP to 21.6 percent of GDP. By contrast, of the so-called emerging economies of the Global South, whose national incomes are much lower, Brazil is closest to the OECD average at just over 15 percent of GDP in 2014 (two thirds of which is spent on pensions in a country with eight persons of working age to one senior citizen), whereas in China in 2009 public social spending amounted to around 7 percent of GDP, comparable to average social spending in the Asia/Pacific region. Public social spending in India (with spending on labor market programmes at 0.6 percent of GDP) is around 3 percent of GDP and around 2 percent in Indonesia is much lower. Public spending in South Africa amounted to around 9 percent of GDP in 2012.[99]

The relatively autonomous capitalist state resting on power-sharing between the working class and the bourgeoisie was consolidated as the working class managed to solve its social problems within the framework of capitalism after WWII. As but one expression of this *embourgeoisement* of metropolitan labor—aside, that is,

---

99 OECD (2014), p. 3.

from its receipt of superwages—welfare policy has been strengthened and intensified over the last century. An early example, as noted above, is the social legislation enacted by chancellor Otto von Bismarck in Germany in the 1880s, intended to dampen the labor militancy of the time. The laws were based on the insurance principle whereby insured workers were entitled to income compensation during unemployment, or as a result of their falling ill. In old age workers would be able to draw from a fund which they themselves contributed to through payroll deduction. Social insurance was the responsibility of both employers and workers and covered the majority of the population. This model has since been continued by all of the subsequent German governments.

The idea that the state was responsible for people's social security and welfare gained ground in all Western European countries in the interwar period. These developed and broadened the functions of the welfare state in the late 1950s, throughout the 1960s, and into the beginning of the 1970s. In Britain and in Scandinavia the welfare state was based on public services paid for by taxes. In Denmark, for instance, major social reform was implemented in 1933 and in 1936, a similar reform, *Folkhemmet* ("the people's home") was established in Sweden. The social democratic welfare state reached its peak in Denmark and Sweden with the proposal of "Economic Democracy" in 1973. This proposal was implemented to a certain extent in Sweden by the Social Democratic Olof Palme government, but was later rolled back under a rising neoliberal consensus. In the UK, the National Health Service Act was adopted in 1948, according to which all British citizens, whether working or not, would be guaranteed income security, health and social care

Table II. Social Expenditure as a Percentage of GDP: Selected OECD Countries, 1980–2014[100]

Year	1980	1985	1990	1995	2000
Australia	10.2	12.1	13.1	16.1	17.2
Belgium	23.5	26	24.9	25.6	24.5
Chile	—	—	9.8	11	12.7
Denmark	24.4	22.9	25	28.7	26
Estonia	—	—	—	—	13.8
Finland	18	22	23.8	29.7	23.3
France	20.6	25.8	24.9	29	28.4
Germany	21.8	22.2	21.4	25.9	26.2
Greece	10.3	16.1	16.5	17.4	19.2
Iceland	—	—	13.5	15	15
Ireland	16	20.8	17.2	17.9	13.1
Israel	—	—	—	16.7	16.8
Italy	18	20.8	21.4	21.7	23.3
Japan	10.3	11.1	11.1	14.1	16.3
Korea	—	—	2.8	3.2	4.8
Mexico	—	1.7	3.2	4.2	5
Netherlands	24.8	25.3	25.6	23.8	19.8
Poland	—	—	14.9	22.3	20.3
Portugal	9.6	10	12.4	16.2	18.6
Spain	15.4	17.6	19.7	21.3	20
Sweden	26	28.2	28.5	31.8	28.2
Turkey	3.1	3.1	5.5	5.6	—
United Kingdom	16.3	19.2	16.3	19.2	18.4
United States	12.8	12.8	13.1	15	14.2
OECD—Total	15.4	17	17.5	19.3	18.6

2005	2009	2010	2011	2012	2013	2014
16.4	17.4	17.2	17.8	18.3	19	19
25.6	29.1	28.8	29.4	30.3	30.9	30.7
8.7	11.2	10.5	10.1	10.2	10	—
27.3	29.7	29.9	30.1	30.2	30.2	30.1
13.1	19.8	18.8	16.8	16.2	16.1	16.3
25	28.3	28.7	28.3	29.4	30.6	31
29.6	31.5	31.7	31.4	31.5	32	31.9
27	27.6	26.8	25.5	25.4	25.6	25.8
21.1	24.4	24.2	25.7	26.1	24.3	24
16.3	18.5	17.9	18.1	17.5	17.1	16.5
15.8	23.4	23.3	22.3	22	21.9	21
16	15.8	15.7	15.6	15.5	15.5	—
24.9	27.8	27.8	27.5	28.1	28.7	28.6
18.4	22	22.1	23.1	—	—	—
6.5	9.4	9	9	9.6	10.2	10.4
6.5	7.7	7.8	7.7	7.9	—	—
21.8	23.1	23.7	23.5	24.1	24.6	24.7
20.7	20.7	20.7	20.1	20.1	20.7	20.6
22.8	25.3	25.2	24.8	24.8	25.8	25.2
20.9	26.1	26.7	26.8	27.1	27.3	26.8
28.7	29.4	27.9	27.2	27.7	28.2	28.1
9.7	13.2	12.6	12.2	12.3	12.5	—
20.2	23.9	22.8	22.7	23	22.5	21.7
15.5	18.5	19.3	19	18.7	18.6	19.2
19.4	21.9	21.7	21.4	21.6	21.7	21.6

services from the state.

Throughout the last century, this form of government became increasingly central to the regulation of the capitalist economy; it was the owner of the civil infrastructure, social institutions, and even some key means of production, so much so that smaller capitalists complained of being "crowded out" of the market. The welfare state is historically based on a substantial public sector. Alongside the development of parliament democracy, therefore, the state ceased to represent the unilateral interests of capital but, rather, capitalist "society" *tout court*. In terms of class struggle, it became to some extent a third party—a broker—between capital and the working class.

Instead of "economic democracy," the Western European trade union movement managed in the coming decades to guarantee to large sections of the working class pensions supplementary to the official state retirement pension. This transpired through the establishment of huge pension fund companies which today are among the largest investors. The pension system has become an important part of the global financial system with investments in stocks and bonds. Functioning entirely on capitalist economic terms, it has further drawn the population of the North closer to the wellspring of imperialist capitalism.

---

100 Organisation for Economic Cooperation and Development (OECD) Statistical Database, online: https://stats.oecd.org/Index.aspx?DataSet-Code=SOCX_AGG. The main social policy areas covered in the OECD Social Expenditure Database (SOCX) are as follows: Old age, Survivors, Incapacity-related benefits, Health, Family, Active labor market programmes, Unemployment, Housing, and Other social policy areas.

There has not been a fundamental difference in policy between liberal or social democratic parties in power in Northwest Europe during the last half century. All parliamentary parties must adapt to the same basic economic policy to ensure jobs, investment, and economic stability within the capitalist world system. The fundamental motor of social change, however, is not parliament but the global economic and political struggles taking place outside of the national electoral system.

Welfare in itself is, of course, not imperialistic, but the welfare state emerged historically in conjunction with imperialism. When the working class and the capitalist class in the North have disputes about the respective shares of wages and profits in national income, about taxation policy, welfare benefits, healthcare, pensions, and so on, it may seem that this has nothing to do with imperialist exploitation, but is purely a matter of domestic policy. However, this is not so; the wages and taxes which pay for social spending are massively inflated by the superexploitation of the proletariat in the Global South. To be sure, this does not mean that it is wrong to defend the principle of free public healthcare, education, pensions, and so on. On the contrary, as well as highlighting the fact that under the current global property dispensation it is only a minority of the working class that is afforded them by virtue of its residence in imperialist countries, the labor internationalist perspective insists that these public goods must be distributed globally.

The existence of the welfare state and the relative rapprochement between the working class and capital does not mean that the class struggle has ended in the North. There is more or less continuous bargaining there over wages and working conditions which can lead to labor unrest and strikes, though these usually end with compromise. Moreover, class struggle takes political form in the North insofar as both capital and organized labor have their representatives in parliament, with each having media platforms and other institutions vying for state power. Yet this class struggle has a limited perspective. It is not about fundamental changes in society, but purely for adjustments to the advantage of each opposing side.

The contradiction between capital and the working class in the imperialist countries is profoundly mitigated by the fact that they stand together in the contradiction between the exploited countries and the imperialist countries. As long as the working class in the imperialist countries sees advantage in the exploitation of the South it will never be able to lead an anti-capitalist class struggle. At the same time, as long as the bourgeoisie can obtain sufficient profits through the exploitation of the Global South it will not force the working class in the North to pursue a radical class struggle. The liberation of the South from imperialism is, therefore, the prerequisite for a change in class relations in the North.

The Welfare State under Pressure

The development of new means of transport, communication, and information technologies combined with neoliberal policies enabled the relocation of industrial production to the Global South. This was driven by the desire for higher profits through the exploitation of cheaper labor, and necessitated by the falling rate of profit in the 1970s. The alternative to this globalization of production incorporating superexploited wage labor would, of course, have been to turn against the working class in the North, with much tougher cuts in welfare and wages than has been the case. This would have ended the social contract that existed between the working class and capital in the First World since WWII and seriously impeded market growth. Such a policy, due also to the parliamentary system, would have been very difficult to implement.

From the late 1970s onwards, the welfare state has come under pressure from neoliberalism. The state is becoming less welfare-oriented and more competitive, to be able to attract capital and employment in the global market. The privatization of the public sector and the outsourcing of public services are in the process of slowly changing the state's character. At the same time, the relocation of production to the South affects class relations in the North in a complex way. Low wages in the South means cheaper goods for the workers of the North as well as higher profits for capital. Both afford the ruling bourgeoisie the wherewithal to maintain the social contract on the home front. However, since the 2007–8 financial crisis rates of profit have been declining. Increased global competition as more and more firms have moved production to the South has put pressure on prices. In addition, the new proletariat in the South is beginning to demand higher wages. The average wage of industrial workers in the export sector in China was about US$2.25 in 2011 compared with US$0.75 per hour in 2005.[101] Finally,

---

101 Pan Kwan Yuk (2013), citing data from Bank of America Merrill Lynch Global Research, Banxico, INEGI, International Labor Organization, and China National Bureau of Statistics.

it has proven difficult for revanchist capital to dissolve the welfare state due to the parliamentary system.

All of this has produced a left tendency in the North's working class: Podemos in Spain, Syriza in Greece, Jeremy Corbyn in the UK, Bernie Sanders in the U.S., Enhedslisten in Denmark, and so on. These have won some support by picking up old social democratic positions. In the short run, their strategy might allow minor improvements for their respective national working classes. However, in a longer and more international perspective, it makes no difference to, and rather tends to obscure, the battle between imperialism and the real proletariat in the South concerning the abolition of capitalism. The only true anti-imperialist socialist strategy is to support that struggle.

What Can Be Done?

There were features of Lenin's time which permitted him to adhere to Engels's description of the difference between the upper strata of the working class—the skilled workers in the exclusive trade unions, in particular—and the lower strata of what both he and Engels called proletarians proper. Consequently, when Lenin looked at Western Europe after WWI, he could only confirm Engels's suggestion that a revolutionary policy must consist in looking askance at the upper strata in the working class movement and turning instead towards the majority of workers, impoverished by the War, who were still definitely proletarian. He realized, of course, that the opportunism of his time, the social democracy of the Second International, had emerged victorious in the Western European labor movement. Opportunists were at the head of the socialist parties and the trade union movement, and Lenin knew that "unless the labour movement rids itself of them, it will remain a bourgeois labour movement."[102] Based on his own experience in Russia, however, he thought that it would be possible for the revolutionary party to wrest leadership of the impoverished *majority* of the proletariat from the opportunists.

Whether or not Lenin's own strategic confidence in the European proletariat was sound, plainly this policy is of no avail in the advanced imperialist countries of today. Much expanded foreign investment in industry and agriculture, unequal trade between rich and poor countries, globalized production chains, and the rise of a "consumer society" in the North—in short, the rapid capitalist development occurring since the Second World War; all of this has created a distinctive situation. In the advanced imperialist countries of today there is no longer an impoverished majority of workers to whom revolutionaries can speak. Rather, virtually all workers in the North rely upon imperialism for their job prospects, their access to public services, their wage rates, their leisure time, and their level and type of political participation.

It is precisely this connection between imperialism and opportunism which we can and should learn from Marx, Engels, and Lenin as the first prerequisite of any meaningful socialist political activity in the wealthiest countries today. Lenin warned against the working-class movement ignoring the imperialist roots of

---

102 Lenin (1964a [1916]). Page 141 in this book.

growing opportunism on the political left. We should not try to cast a veil over reality. It is abundantly clear to us that it is only the anti-capitalist and anti-imperialist struggle in the South that will either break up the monopoly of the advanced capitalist world or cause this very world to end in deadlock. Only the liberation struggles of the Global South can create a social situation in which the working class of the Global North will listen to and understand socialist internationalism. This does not make the cause hopeless. However, as many Marxists have stressed, it does make it much more difficult for the workers of the West to carry out revolution.

Initially, we can only hope to reach and mobilize a minority for an anti-imperialist strategy in the North. Such a strategy will not be aimed at a radical change in the social system in the North, but to provide political and material support to the proletarian struggle in the South, which has a fundamental and pressing interest in a different world order. It is a vital task for anti-imperialists in the North to try to prevent imperialist intervention, by weakening imperialism on its home turf, and by fighting against social-chauvinism, racism, and national egoism to avoid the development of a fascist-based people's imperialism in the North.

Before the immediate tasks of revolutionaries in imperialist countries can be determined in greater detail a number of questions must be answered. Lenin defined the task of the revolutionaries in the West as follows: "To be able to seek, find and correctly determine the specific path, or the particular turn of events that will *lead* the masses to the real, decisive and final revolutionary struggle."[103]

---

103 Lenin (1964b), p. 97.

Therefore, the task facing socialists in 2016 may rather be said to consist in seeking and finding the path, the turn of events, which will recreate such "masses," re-create this proletariat proper in the Western world. One thing is certain: in order to carry out revolutionary activity in the advanced capitalist countries today it is more than ever necessary to have a well-founded knowledge of all classes in all countries of major importance, of the most important economic trends not only where we live, and certainly not only in the imperialist world in general, or in China, South Africa, or Brazil, but in all parts of the world.

Conclusion

The struggle against imperialism worldwide and the struggle against fascism and racism in the imperialist countries (the ideological and political bedrocks of imperialist capitalism in a time of crisis) are at the cutting edge of the socialist movement at the present conjuncture.

The population of the Global North is living well beyond its means. It is living off surplus (value) extorted from the workers and peasants of the Global South. Are First World workers prepared to install a government that will socialize industry, plan investment, redistribute wealth according to labor provided and human need; re-engage in productive labor *en masse*; trade fairly with the nations of the Global South and remove their military presence from them; and accept a decline in living standards until such time as their own productivity and the well-being of the planet allows them to resume their current affluence? Or, instead, will they allow themselves to be pacified by governments that allow for a modicum of wealth redistribution but involve themselves in ramping-up imperialist exploitation and aggression throughout the world? In the absence of a coherent socialist internationalism on the ostensible left, it seems likely that jingoism, war-mongering, and right-wing populism will gain further traction in the years to come. Nonetheless, an appeal to reason, compassion, and solidarity, rather than simply the wallet, must make some impact if only the "left" were brave enough to prioritise it. Meanwhile, it is increasingly in the interests of all oppressed "minorities" and progressive people to organise against actually existing fascism and the threat of more to come.

Will the social preconditions of revolution be created only when the imperialist exploitation of the South is impeded? Will new imperialist or inter-imperialist wars create a revolutionary situation? Will the destruction of the ecological balance and climate change create social conditions that call for "lifeboat socialism"? Alternatively, perhaps a combination of these factors will lead to social change that will benefit the overwhelming majority of humanity. It may still take quite a long time before the arrival of the revolutionary situation—but things may also run fast.

Bibliography:

Aidat, Dipa Nusantara. 1964. *Set Afire the Banteng Spirit! Ever Forward, No Retreat!* Peking: Foreign Language Press.

Anievas, Alexander. 2015. "Marxist Theory and the Origins of the First World War." In: Alexander Anievas, Editor. *Cataclysm 1914: The First World War and the Making of Modern World Politics.* Leiden: Brill, 96–143.

Bashear, Suliman. 1980. *Communism in the Arab East.* London: Ithaca Press.

Bell, Duncan. 2007. *The Idea of Greater Britain: Empire and the Future of World Order, 1860–1900.* New Jersey: Princeton University Press.

Bennigsen, Alexandre. 1958. "Sultan Galiev: The USSR and the Colonial Revolution." In: Walter Laqueur, Editor. *The Middle East in Transition.* London: Routledge & Kegan Paul, 398–414.

Bukharin, Nikolai. No Date [1915 and 1917]. *Imperialism and World Economy.* London: Martin and Lawrence.

—— 1956 [1925]. Extracts from the Theses of the Fifth ECCI Plenum on the Peasant Question, 21 March–6 April. In: Jane Degras, Editor. *The Communist International, 1919–1943: Selected Documents, Vol. 2, 1923–1928.* Oxford: Oxford University Press.

Burleigh, Michael and Wolfgang Wippermann. 2011 [1991]. *The Racial State: Germany 1933–1945*. Cambridge: Cambridge University Press.

Cave Brown, Anthony and Charles B. Macdonald. 1981. *On a Field of Red: The Communist International and the Coming of World War II*. New York: G. P. Putnam's Sons.

Clough, Robert. 1992. *Labor: A Party Fit For Imperialism*. London: Larkin Publications.

Cobban, Alfred. 1965. *A History of Modern France. Vol. 3. 1871–1962*. London: Penguin.

Cope, Zak. 2008. *Dimensions of Prejudice: Towards a Political Economy of Bigotry*. Bern, Switzerland: Peter Lang.

—— 2015. *Divided World Divided Class: Global Political Economy and the Stratification of Labor under Capitalism*. Montreal: Kersplebedeb.

—— 2015a. "German Imperialism and Social Imperialism, 1871–1933." 2015. In: Immanuel Ness and Zak Cope, Editors. *The Palgrave Encyclopedia of Imperialism and Anti-Imperialism*. Basingstoke: Palgrave Macmillan, 652–666.

Copping, Jasper. 2012. "British have invaded nine out of ten countries—so look out Luxembourg." *Telegraph*, November 4. Online: http://www.telegraph.co.uk/history/9653497/British-have-invaded-nine-out-of-ten-countries-so-look-out-Luxembourg.html

Daniels, R. V., Editor. 1994. *A Documentary History of Communism and the World. From Revolution to Collapse.* Third Edition. Hanover, New Haven: University Press of New England.

Degras, Jane, Editor. 1960. *The Communist International, 1919–1943: Selected Documents, Vol. 2, 1923–1928.* Oxford: Oxford University Press.

Dimitrov, Georgi. 1973 [1935]. *Report to the 7th Congress of the Communist International: For the unity of the Working Class against Fascism.* London: Red Star Press.

Duiker, Walter J. 2000. *Ho Chi Minh: A Life.* New York: Hyperion.

Dutt, Rajani Palme. 1940. *India Today.* London: Left Book Club.

Edwards, H. W. 1978. *Labor Aristocracy: Mass Base of Social Democracy.* Stockholm: Aurora.

Eley, Geoff. 2015. "Germany, the Fischer Controversy, and the Context of War: Rethinking German Imperialism, 1880–1914." In: Alexander Anievas, Editor. *Cataclysm 1914: The First World War and the Making of Modern World Politics.* Leiden: Brill, 23–46.

Engels, Friedrich. 2010 [1884]. *Origins of the Family, Private Property, and the State.* London: Penguin.

Goebel, Michael. 2015. *A Parisian Ho Chi Minh Trail: Writing Global History through Interwar Paris*. Online: https://imperialglobalexeter.com/2015/12/07/10-a-parisian-ho-chi-minh-trail-writing-global-history-through-interwar-paris/

—— 2015a. *Anti-Imperial Metropolis: Interwar Paris and the Seeds of Third World Nationalism*. Cambridge: Cambridge University Press.

Harsch, Donna. 1993. *German Social Democracy and the Rise of Nazism*. North Carolina: University of North Carolina Press.

Heartfield, James and Kevin Rooney. 2015. *Who's Afraid of the Easter Rising?* Winchester, UK: Zero Books.

Hitler, Adolf. 1939 [1925]. *Mein Kampf*. London: Hurst and Blackett Ltd.

Hô Chí Minh. 1962. "The Path Which Led Me to Leninism." Originally published in the Soviet review *Problems of the East* on the occasion of the 90th anniversary of V.I. Lenin's birthday, April 1960. In *Selected Works of Ho Chi Minh*, Vol. 4. Hanoi: Foreign Languages Publishing House. Online: https://www.marxists.org/reference/archive/ho-chi-minh/works/1960/04/x01.htm

—— 1960 [1924]. "Report on the National and Colonial Questions at the Fifth Congress of the Communist International, July 8, 1924." In: *Selected Works of Ho Chi Minh*, Vol. 1. Hanoi: Foreign Languages Publishing House.

Hobson, John A. 1968 [1902]. *Imperialism: A Study*. London: George Allen and Unwin Ltd.

Jessop, Bob. 2002. *The Future of the Capitalist State*. Cambridge: Polity Press.

Johnson, Chalmers. 1973. *Autopsy on People's War*. California: University of California Press.

Kelly, M.G.E. 2015. *Biopolitical Imperialism*. Winchester, UK: Zero Books.

Kerswell, Timothy. 2011. *The Global Division of Labor and the Division in Global Labor*. Doctoral Thesis. Queensland University of Technology, School of Humanities and Human Services, Australia. Online: http://eprints.qut.edu.au/46838/1/Timothy_Kerswell_Thesis.pdf

Krooth, Richard. 1980. *Arms and Empire: Imperial Patterns before World War II*. Santa Barbara, CA: Harvest Press.

Kuhn, Gabriel. 2014. *Turning Money into Rebellion: The Unlikely Story of Denmark's Revolutionary Bank Robbers*. Oakland, California and Montreal, Quebec: PM Press and Kersplebedeb.

Kumm, Björn. 2013. *Motstand*. Lund: Historska Media.

Lacouture, Jean. 1968. *Ho Chi Minh: A Political Biography*. New York: Vintage.

League of Nations. 1926. "Memo on Production and Trade." In: *International Economic Conference*. Economic and Financial Section. Geneva: League of Nations, 9–20.

Lenin, Vladimir Ilyich. 1964 [1916]. "Imperialism and the Split in Socialism." Originally published in *Sbornik Sotsial-Demokrata*, no. 2, December. In *Collected Works*, Vol. 23. Moscow: Progress Publishers, 105–120.

—— 1964a [1917]. "The State and Revolution." In *Collected Works*, Vol. 25. Moscow: Progress Publishers, 381–492.

—— 1964b [1920]. "'Left-Wing' Communism: An Infantile Disorder." Originally published as a pamphlet, May 1920. In *Collected Works*, Vol. 31. Moscow: Progress Publisher, 17–118.

—— 1965 [1920]. "Draft Theses on the National and Colonial Questions for the Second Congress of the Communist International." Originally published in June 1920. In *Collected Works*, Vol. 31. Moscow: Progress Publishers, 144–151.

—— 1965b [1920]. "Report of the Commission on the National and Colonial Questions, July 26. The Second Congress of the Communist International, July 19–August 7, 1920." Originally published in 1921 in the book *The Second Congress of the Communist International, Verbatim Report*. In *Collected Works*, Vol. 31. Moscow: Progress Publishers, 213–263.

—— 1968. "Notebooks on Imperialism." In *Collected Works*, Vol. 39. Moscow: Progress Publishers.

—— 1972 [1907]. "The International Socialist Congress in Stuttgart." Originally published in *Proletary*, no. 17, October 20, 1907. In *Collected Works*, Vol. 13. Moscow: Progress Publishers, 75–81.

—— 1972a [1917]. "Revision of the Party Programme." Originally published in the journal *Prosveshcheniye*, no. 1–2, October. In *Collected Works*, Vol. 26. Moscow: Progress Publishers, 149–178.

—— 1972b [1918]. "Political Report of the 7th Committee. Extraordinary Seventh Congress of the R.C.P.(B.), March 6–8, 1918." Originally published in full in 1923 in the book *Seventh Congress of the Russian Communist Party. Verbatim Report*. In *Collected Works*, Vol. 27. Moscow: Progress Publishers, 85–158.

—— 1974 [1915]. "The Collapse of the Second International." Originally published in the journal *Kommunist*, no. 1–2. In *Collected Works*, Vol. 21. Moscow: Progress Publishers, 205–259.

Losurdo, Domenico. 2013. *La Lotta di Classe: Una Storia Politica e Filosofica*. Roma-Bari: Laterza.

Luxemburg, Rosa. 1951 [1913]. *The Accumulation of Capital*. London: Routledge and Kegan Paul.

Marx, Karl. 1959 [1871]. "The Civil War in France." In Lewis
S. Feuer, Editor. *Marx and Engels: Basic Writings on Politics
and Philosophy.* New York, Doubleday, 362–75.

—— 2000. [1850]. "The Class Struggles in France, 1848 to
1850." Originally published in the *Neue Rheinische Zeitung
Revue*, October 1850. In David McLellan, Editor. *Karl
Marx: Selected Writings.* Oxford: Oxford University Press,
313–26.

Marx, Karl and Friedrich Engels. 2016. *Selected Texts On
Colonialism, Industrial Monopoly and the Working Class
Movement.* Edited by Torkil Lauesen with an Introduction
by Torkil Lauesen and Zak Cope. Montreal: Kersplebedeb.

—— 1963. *Marx and Engels on Britain.* Moscow: Progress
Publishers.

—— 1969 [1848]. *Manifesto of the Communist Party.* In Marx
and Engels, *Selected Works*, Vol. I. Moscow: Progress
Publishers, 98–137.

Matsumura, Wendy. 2015. "The Expansion of the Japanese
Empire and the Rise of the Global Agrarian Question
after the First World War." In Alexander Anievas, Editor.
*Cataclysm 1914: The First World War and the Making of
Modern World Politics.* Leiden: Brill, 144–173.

Meisner, Maurice. 1970. *Li Ta-chao and the Origins of Chinese
Marxism.* New York: Atheneum.

Nehru, Jawaharlal. 1953 [1936]. *An Autobiography with musings on recent events in India*. London: The Bodley Head.

Nguyen Ai Quoc. 1974 [1924]. "The struggle Against Capitalism Lies in the Colonies." In Helmut Gruber, Editor. *Soviet Russia Masters the Comintern: International Communism in the Era of Stalin's Ascendancy*. New York: Doubleday.

Organization for Economic Cooperation and Development (OECD). 2014. "Social Expenditure Update. Social spending is falling in some countries, but in many others it remains at historically high levels." November. Online: http://www.oecd.org/els/soc/OECD2014-Social-Expenditure-Update-Nov2014-8pages.pdf

Pan Kwan Yuk. 2013. "Mexican Labor Cheaper Than China." *Financial Times*. April 5. Online: http://blogs.ft.com/beyond-brics/2013/04/05/made-in-mexico-now-cheaper-than-china.

Pauwels, Jacques. 2016. *The Great Class War 1914–1918*. Toronto: Lorimer.

Petersson, Fredrik. 2013. *"We Are Neither Visionaries Nor Utopian Dreamers": Willi Münzenberg, the League against Imperialism, and the Comintern, 1925–1933*. Doctoral dissertation. Åbo Akademi University, Finland. Online: http://www.doria.fi/bitstream/handle/10024/90023/petersson_fredrik.pdf.

Poulantzas, Nicos. 1978. *Political Power and Social Classes.* London: New Left Books.

Prandy, K., A. Stewart, and R. M. Blackburn. 1983. *White Collar Unionism.* London: Macmillan.

Redfern, Neil. 2005. *Class or Nation: Communists, Imperialism and Two World Wars.* London: Tauris Academic Studies.

Roberts, Glenn L. 2007. *Commissar and Mullah: Soviet-Muslim Policy from 1917 to 1924.* Boca Raton, Florida: Dissertation. Com.

Rustamova-Tohidi, Solmaz. 1996. "The First Congress of the Peoples of the East: Aims, Tasks, Results." In Mikhail Narinsky and Jürgen Rojahn, Editors. *Centre and Periphery: The History of the Comintern in the Light of New Documents.* Amsterdam: International Institute of Social History, 74–80.

Schevill, Ferdinand. 1951. *A History of Europe.* New York: Harcourt, Brace and Co.

Smith, Aubrey Douglas. 1942. *Guilty Germans?* London: Victor Gollancz.

Sternberg, Frtiz. 1935. *Der Faschismus an der Macht.* Amsterdam: Contact.

Sultan-Galiev, Mirsaid. 1979 [1919]. "The Social Revolution and the East." Originally published in *Žizn' nacional'nostej,* Vol. 38, no. 46. In Alexandre Bennigsen and S. Enders

Wimbush. *Muslim National Communism in the Soviet Union.* Chicago: University of Chicago Press.

Wadsworth, Marc. 1998. *Comrade Sak: A Political Biography.* Leeds: Peepal Tree.

Weiner, Michael. 1996. "Comintern in East Asia." In Kevin McDermott and Jeremy Agnew, Editors. *The Comintern: A History of International Communism from Lenin to Stalin.* Basingstoke: Macmillan Press.

World Health Organisation. 2014. *World Health Statistics 2014.* Geneva: United Nations.

Worley, Matthew. 2002. *Class against Class: The Communist Party in Britain between the Wars.* London: I. B. Tauris.

Zinoviev, Grigory. 1942 [1916]. "The Social Roots of Opportunism." Originally published in *The War and the Crisis in Socialism*, 1916. Subsequently published in *New International*, *Vol. 8*, nos. 2–5, March–June 1942.

Review: J. A. Hobson:
The Evolution of Modern Capitalism

Written April 1899. Published in May 1899 in the journal Nachalo
No. 5.

... The last chapter of Hobson's book, "Civilisation and Industrial Development," is perhaps the best. In this chapter the author proves by a number of very apt arguments the need to reform the modern industrial system along the line of expanding "public control" and the "socialisation of industry." In evaluating Hobson's somewhat optimistic views regarding the methods by which these "reforms" can be brought about, the special features of English history and of English life must be borne in mind: the high development of democracy, the absence of militarism, the enormous strength of the organised trade unions, the growing investment of English capital outside of England, which weakens the antagonism between the English employers and workers, etc. ...

Lenin Collected Works, Vol. 4, p. 102

The International Socialist Congress in Stuttgart

Written August–September 1907. Published in Proletary *No. 17, October 20, 1907.*

... This is not the first time the colonial question has figured at international congresses. Up till now their decisions have always been an unqualified condemnation of bourgeois colonial policy as a policy of plunder and violence. This time, however, the Congress Commission was so composed that opportunist elements, headed by Van Kol of Holland, predominated in it. A sentence was inserted in the draft resolution to the effect that the Congress did not in principle condemn all colonial policy, for under socialism colonial policy could play a civilising role. The minority in the Commission (Ledebour of Germany, the Polish and Russian Social-Democrats, and many others) vigorously protested against any such idea being entertained. The matter was referred to Congress, where the forces of the two trends were found to be so nearly equal that there was an extremely heated debate.

The opportunists rallied behind Van Kol. Speaking for the majority of the German delegation Bernstein and David urged acceptance of a "socialist colonial policy" and fulminated against the radicals for their barren, negative attitude, their failure to appreciate the importance of reforms, their lack of a practical colonial programme, etc. Incidentally, they were opposed by Kautsky, who felt compelled to ask the Congress to pronounce *against* the majority of the German delegation. He rightly pointed out that there was no question of rejecting the struggle for reforms; that was

The proletarians of the ancient world, this saying runs, lived at the expense of society; modern society lives at the expense of the proletarians.

explicitly stated in other sections of the resolution, which had evoked no dispute. The point at issue was whether we should make concessions to the modern regime of bourgeois plunder and violence. The Congress was to discuss present-day colonial policy, which was based on the downright enslavement of primitive populations. The bourgeoisie was actually introducing slavery in the colonies and subjecting the native populations to unprecedented outrages and acts of violence, "civilising" them by the spread of liquor and syphilis. And in that situation socialists were expected to utter evasive phrases about the possibility of accepting colonial policy in principle! That would be an outright desertion to the bourgeois point of view. It would be a decisive step towards subordinating the proletariat to bourgeois ideology, to bourgeois imperialism, which is now arrogantly raising its head.

The Congress defeated the Commission's motion by 128 votes to 108 with ten abstentions (Switzerland). It should be noted that at Stuttgart, for the first time, each nation was allotted a definite number of votes, varying from twenty (for the big nations, Russia included) to two (Luxembourg). The combined vote of the small nations, which either do not pursue a colonial policy, or which suffer from it, outweighed the vote of nations where even the proletariat has been somewhat infected with the lust of conquest.

This vote on the colonial question is of very great importance. First, it strikingly showed up socialist opportunism, which succumbs to bourgeois blandishments. Secondly, it revealed a negative feature in the European labour movement, one that can do no little harm to the proletarian cause, and for that reason should receive serious attention. Marx frequently quoted a very significant saying of Sismondi. The proletarians of the ancient world, this saying runs, lived at the expense of society; modern society lives at the expense of the proletarians.

The non-propertied, but non-working, class is incapable of overthrowing the exploiters. Only the proletarian class, which maintains the whole of society, can bring about the social revolution. However, as a result of the extensive colonial policy, the European proletarian *partly* finds himself in a position when it is *not* his labour, but the labour of the practically enslaved natives in the colonies, that maintains the whole of society. The British bourgeoisie, for example, derives more profit from the many millions of the population of India and other colonies than from the British workers. In certain countries this provides the material and economic basis for infecting the proletariat with colonial chauvinism. Of course, this may be only a temporary phenomenon, but the evil must nonetheless be clearly realised and its causes understood in order to be able to rally the proletariat of all countries for the struggle against such opportunism. This struggle is bound to be victorious, since the "privileged" nations are a diminishing faction of the capitalist nations. ...

Lenin Collected Works, Vol. 13, pp. 75–77

In America

Written December 1912. Published in Kommunist *No. 6.*

The state of affairs in the American labour movement shows us, as it does in Britain, the remarkably clear-cut division between purely trade unionist and socialist strivings, the split between bourgeois labour policy and socialist labour policy. For, strange as it may seem, in capitalist society even the working class can carry on a bourgeois policy, if it forgets about its emancipatory aims, puts up with wage-slavery and confines itself to seeking alliances now with one bourgeois party, now with another, for the sake of imaginary "improvements" in its indentured condition.

The principal historical cause of the particular prominence and (temporary) strength of bourgeois labour policy in Britain and America is the long-standing political liberty and the exceptionally favourable conditions, in comparison with other countries, for the deep-going and widespread development of capitalism. These conditions have tended to produce within the working class an aristocracy that has trailed behind the bourgeoisie, betraying its own class.

In the twentieth century, this peculiar situation in Britain and America is rapidly disappearing. Other countries are catching up with Anglo-Saxon capitalism, and the mass of workers are learning about socialism at first hand. The faster the growth of world capitalism, the sooner will socialism triumph in America and Britain.

Lenin Collected Works, Vol. 36, pp. 214–215

In Britain (The Sad Results of Opportunism)

Published in Pravda *No. 85, April 12, 1913.*

The British Labour Party, which must be distinguished from the *two* socialist parties in Britain, the British Socialist Party and the Independent Labour Party, is the workers' organisation that is most opportunist and soaked in the spirit of liberal-labour policy.

In Britain there is full political liberty and the socialist parties exist quite openly. But the Labour Party is the parliamentary representative of workers' organisations, of which some are non-political, and others liberal, a regular mixture of the kind our liquidators want, those who hurl so much abuse at the "underground."

The opportunism of the British Labour Party is to be explained by the specific historical conditions of the latter half of the nineteenth century in Britain, when the "aristocracy of labour" shared to some extent in the particularly high profits of British capital. Now these conditions are becoming a thing of the past. Even the Independent Labour Party, i.e., the *socialist* opportunists in Britain, realises that the Labour Party has landed in a morass.

In the last issue of *The Labour Leader*, the organ of the Independent Labour Party, we find the following edifying communication. Naval estimates are being discussed in the British Parliament. The socialists introduce a motion to *reduce* them. The bourgeoisie, of course, quash it by voting *for* the government.

And the Labour M.P.s?

Fifteen vote for the reduction, i.e., against the government; 21 *are absent*; 4 vote *for the government*, i.e., against the reduction!

Two of the four try to justify their action on the grounds that the workers in their constituencies earn their living in the armament industries.

There you have a striking example of how opportunism leads to the *betrayal* of socialism, the *betrayal* of the workers' cause. As we have already indicated, condemnation of this treachery is spreading ever wider among British socialists. From the example of other people's mistakes, the Russian workers, too, should learn to understand how fatal are opportunism and liberal-labour policy.

Lenin Collected Works, Vol. 19, pp. 55–56

The opportunism of the British Labour Party is to be explained by the specific historical conditions of the latter half of the nineteenth century in Britain, when the "aristocracy of labour" shared to some extent in the particularly high profits of British capital.

Karl Marx

Written July–November 1914. Published in Granat Encyclopedia, *7th edition, Vol. 28.*

… The fundamental task of proletarian tactics was defined by Marx in strict conformity with all the postulates of his materialist-dialectical *Weltanschauung*. Only an objective consideration of the sum total of the relations between absolutely all the classes in a given society, and consequently a consideration of the objective stage of development reached by that society and of the relations between it and other societies, can serve as a basis for the correct tactics of an advanced class. At the same time, all classes and all countries are regarded, not statically, but dynamically, i.e., not in a state of immobility, but in motion (whose laws are determined by the economic conditions of existence of each class). Motion, in its turn, is regarded from the standpoint, not only of the past, but also of the future, and that not in the vulgar sense it is understood in by the "evolutionists,"

All this should be compared with numerous references by Marx and Engels to the example of the British labour movement, showing how industrial "prosperity" leads to attempts "to buy the proletariat," to divert them from the struggle; how this prosperity in general "demoralises the workers"; how the British proletariat becomes "bourgeoisified"

who see only slow changes, but dialectically: "… in developments of such magnitude twenty years are no more than a day," Marx wrote to Engels, "though later on there may come days in which twenty years are embodied."

At each stage of development, at each moment, proletarian tactics must take account of this objectively inevitable dialectics of human history, on the one hand, utilising the periods of political stagnation or of sluggish, so-called "peaceful" development in order to develop the class-consciousness, strength and militancy of the advanced class, and, on the other hand, directing all the work of this utilisation towards the "ultimate aim" of that class's advance, towards creating in it the ability to find practical solutions for great tasks in the great days, in which "twenty years are embodied." Two of Marx's arguments are of special importance in this connection: one of these is contained in *The Poverty of Philosophy* and concerns the economic struggle and economic organisations of the proletariat; the other is contained in the *Communist Manifesto* and concerns the political tasks of the proletariat. The former runs as follows:

> Large-scale industry concentrates in one place a crowd of people unknown to one another. Competition divides their interests. But the maintenance of wages, this common interest which they have against their boss, unites them in a common thought of resistance—combination … . Combinations, at first isolated, constitute themselves into groups … and in face of always united capital, the maintenance of the association becomes more necessary to them (i.e., the workers) than that of wages. … In this struggle—a veritable war—all the elements

necessary for a coming battle unite and develop. Once it has reached this point, association takes on a political character.

Here we have the programme and tactics of the economic struggle and of the trade union movement for several decades to come, for all the lengthy period in which the proletariat will prepare its forces for the "coming battle." All this should be compared with numerous references by Marx and Engels to the example of the British labour movement, showing how industrial "prosperity" leads to attempts "to buy the proletariat," to divert them from the struggle; how this prosperity in general "demoralises the workers"; how the British proletariat becomes "bourgeoisified"—"this most bourgeois of all nations is apparently aiming ultimately at the possession of a bourgeois aristocracy and a bourgeois proletariat alongside the bourgeoisie"; how its "revolutionary energy" oozes away; how it will be necessary to wait a more or less lengthy space of time before "the British workers will free themselves from their apparent bourgeois infection"; how the British labour movement "lacks the mettle of the Chartists"; how the British workers' leaders are becoming a type midway between "a radical bourgeois and a worker"; how, owing to Britain's monopoly, and as long as that monopoly lasts, "the British workingman will not budge." The tactics of the economic struggle, in connection with the general course *(and outcome)* of the working-class movement, are considered here from a remarkably broad, comprehensive, dialectical, and genuinely revolutionary standpoint. ...

Lenin Collected Works, Vol. 21, pp. 75–76

The Collapse of the Second International

Written May–June 1915. First published in 1915 in Kommunist
No. 1–2.

... By social-chauvinism we mean acceptance of the idea of the defence
of the fatherland in the present imperialist war, justification of an
alliance between socialists and the bourgeoisie and the governments of their "own" countries in this war, a refusal to propagate
and support proletarian-revolutionary action against one's "own"
bourgeoisie, etc. It is perfectly obvious that social-chauvinism's basic
ideological and political content fully coincides with the foundations
of opportunism. It is *one and the same* tendency. In the conditions of
the war of 1914–15, opportunism leads to social-chauvinism. The
idea of class collaboration is opportunism's main feature. The war
has brought this idea to its logical conclusion, and has augmented
its usual factors and stimuli with a number of extraordinary ones;
through the operation of special threats and coercion it has compelled the philistine and disunited masses to collaborate with the
bourgeoisie. This circumstance has naturally multiplied adherents
of opportunism and fully explains why many radicals of yesterday
have deserted to that camp.

Opportunism means sacrificing the fundamental interests of
the masses to the temporary interests of an insignificant minority
of the workers or, in other words, an alliance between a section of
the workers and the bourgeoisie, directed against the mass of the
proletariat. The war has made such an alliance particularly conspic-
uous and inescapable. Opportunism was engendered in the course
of decades by the special features in the period of the development

Opportunism means sacrificing the fundamental interests of the masses to the temporary interests of an insignificant minority of the workers or, in other words, an alliance between a section of the workers and the bourgeoisie, directed against the mass of the proletariat.

of capitalism, when the comparatively peaceful and cultured life of a stratum of privileged workingmen "bourgeoisified" them, gave them crumbs from the table of their national capitalists, and isolated them from the suffering, misery and revolutionary temper of the impoverished and ruined masses. The imperialist war is the direct continuation and culmination of this state of affairs, because this is a war for the *privileges* of the Great Power nations, for the repartition of colonies, and domination over other nations. To defend and strengthen their privileged position as a petty-bourgeois "upper stratum" or aristocracy (and bureaucracy) of the working class—such is the natural wartime continuation of petty-bourgeois opportunist hopes and the corresponding tactics, such is the economic foundation of present-day social-imperialism. And, of course, the force of habit, the routine of relatively "peaceful" evolution, national prejudices, a fear of sharp turns and a disbelief in them—all these were additional circumstances which enhanced both opportunism and a hypocritical and a craven reconciliation with opportunism—ostensibly only for a time and only because of extraordinary causes and motives. The war has changed this opportunism, which had been fostered for decades, raised it to a higher stage, increased the number and the variety of its shades, augmented the ranks of its adherents, enriched their arguments with a multitude of new sophisms, and has merged, so to say, many new streams and rivulets with the mainstream of opportunism. However, the mainstream has not disappeared. Quite the reverse.

Social-chauvinism is an opportunism which has matured to such a degree that the *continued* existence of this bourgeois abscess within the socialist parties has become impossible.

Those who refuse to see the closest and unbreakable link between social-chauvinism and opportunism clutch at individual instances—this opportunist or another, they say, has turned internationalist; this radical or another has turned chauvinist. But this kind of argument carries no weight as far as the development of *trends* is concerned. Firstly, chauvinism and opportunism in the labour movement have the same economic basis: the alliance between a numerically small upper stratum of the proletariat and the petty bourgeoisie—who get but morsels of the privileges of their "own" national capital—against the masses of the proletarians, the masses of the toilers and the oppressed in general. Secondly, the two trends have the same ideological and political content. Thirdly, the old division of socialists into an opportunist trend and a revolutionary, which was characteristic of the period of the Second International (1889–1914), *corresponds,* by and large, to the new division into chauvinists and internationalists. ...

Lenin Collected Works, Vol. 21, pp. 242–244

The Question of Peace

Written July–August 1915. First published in 1924.

... Let us see how this question should be posed by socialists.

The peace slogan can be advanced either in connection with definite peace terms, or without any conditions at all, as a struggle, not for a definite kind of peace, but for peace in general (*Frieden ohne weiters*). In the latter case, we obviously have a slogan that is not only non-socialist but entirely devoid of meaning and content. Most people are definitely in favour of peace in general, including even Kirchener, Joffre, Hindenburg, and Nicholas the Bloodstained, for *each* of them wants an end to the war. The trouble is that every one of them advances peace terms that are imperialist (i.e., predatory and oppressive, towards other peoples), and to the advantage of his "own" nation. Slogans must be brought forward so as to enable the masses, through propaganda and agitation, to see the unbridgeable distinction between socialism and capitalism (imperialism), and *not* for the purpose of *reconciling two* hostile classes and two hostile political lines, with the aid of a formula that "unites" the most different things.

To continue: can the socialists of different countries be united on definite *terms* of peace? If so, such terms must undoubtedly include the recognition of the right to self-determination for all nations, and also renunciation of all "annexations," i.e., infringements of that right. If, however, that right is recognised only for *some* nations, then you are defending the *privileges* of certain nations, i.e., you are a nationalist and imperialist, not a socialist. If, however, that right is recognised for *all* nations, then you cannot single

Slogans must be brought forward so as to enable the masses, through propaganda and agitation, to see the unbridgeable distinction between socialism and capitalism (imperialism), and not for the purpose of reconciling two hostile classes and two hostile political lines, with the aid of a formula that "unites" the most different things.

out Belgium alone, for instance; you must take all the oppressed peoples, both in Europe (the Irish in Britain, the Italians in Nice, the Danes in Germany, fifty-seven per cent of Russia's population, etc.) and *outside of Europe*, i.e., all colonies. Comrade A. P. has done well to remind us of them. Britain, France, and Germany have a total population of some one hundred and fifty million, whereas the populations they oppress in the colonies number over four hundred million! The essence of the imperialist war, i.e., a war waged for the interests of the capitalists, consists, not only in the war being waged with the aim of oppressing new nations, of carving up the colonies, but also in its being waged primarily by the advanced nations, which oppress a number of other peoples comprising the majority of the earth's population.

The German Social-Democrats, who justify the seizure of Belgium or reconcile themselves to it, are actually imperialists and nationalists, not Social-Democrats, since they defend the "right" of the German bourgeoisie (partly also of the German workers) to oppress the Belgians, the Alsatians, the Danes, the Poles, the Negroes in Africa, etc. They are not socialists, but *menials* to the German bourgeoisie, whom they are aiding to rob other nations. The Belgian socialists who demand the liberation and indemnification of Belgium *alone* are also actually defending a demand of the Belgian bourgeoisie, who would go on plundering the 15,000,000 Congolese population and obtaining concessions and privileges in other countries. The Belgian bourgeoisie's foreign investments amount to something like three thousand million francs. Safeguarding the profits from these investments by using every kind of fraud and machinations is the real "national interest" of "gallant Belgium." The same applies in a still greater degree to Russia, Britain, France and Japan.

It follows that if the demand for the freedom of nations is not to be a false phrase covering up the imperialism and the nationalism of *certain individual countries*, it must be extended to all peoples and to all colonies. Such a demand, however, is obviously meaningless *unless* it is accompanied by a series of revolutions in all the advanced countries. Moreover, it cannot be accomplished without a successful socialist revolution.

...

The slogan of self-determination of nations should also be advanced in *connection* with the imperialist era of capitalism. We do not stand for the status quo, or for the philistine Utopia of *standing aside* in great wars. We stand for a revolutionary struggle against imperialism, i.e., capitalism. Imperialism consists in a striving of nations that oppress a number of other nations to extend and increase that oppression and to repartition the colonies. That is why the question of self-determination of nations today *hinges* on the conduct of socialists of the *oppressor* nations. A socialist of any of the *oppressor* nations (Britain, France, Germany, Japan, Russia, the United States of America, etc.) who does not recognise and does not struggle for the right of oppressed nations to self-determination (i.e., the right to secession) is in reality a chauvinist, not a socialist.

Only this point of view can lead to a sincere and consistent struggle against imperialism, to a proletarian, not a philistine approach (today) to the national question. Only this point of view can lead to a consistent application of the principle of combating any form of the oppression of nations; it removes mistrust among the proletarians of the oppressor and oppressed nations, makes for a united international struggle for the socialist revolution (i.e., for the only accomplishable regime of complete national

> **A socialist of any of the oppressor nations (Britain, France, Germany, Japan, Russia, the United States of America, etc.) who does not recognise and does not struggle for the right of oppressed nations to self-determination (i.e., the right to secession) is in reality a chauvinist, not a socialist.**

equality), as distinct from the philistine Utopia of freedom for all small states in general, under capitalism.

This is the point of view adopted by our Party, i.e., by those Social-Democrats of Russia who have rallied around the Central Committee. This was the point of view adopted by Marx when he taught the proletariat that "no nation can be free if it oppresses other nations." It was from this point of view that Marx demanded the separation of Ireland from Britain, this in the interests of the freedom movement, not only of the Irish, but especially of the *British* workers.

If the socialists of Britain do not recognise and uphold Ireland's right to secession, if the French do not do the same for Italian Nice, the Germans for Alsace-Lorraine, Danish Schleswig, and Poland, the Russians for Poland, Finland, the Ukraine, etc., and the Poles for the Ukraine—if all the socialists of the "Great" Powers, i.e., the great robber powers, do not uphold that right in respect of the colonies, it is solely because they are in fact imperialists, not socialists. It is ridiculous to cherish illusions that people who do not fight for "the right to self-determination" of the oppressed nations, while they themselves belong to the oppressor nations, are capable of practising socialist policies.

Instead of leaving it to the hypocritical phrase-mongers to deceive the people by phrases and promises concerning the possibility of a democratic peace, socialists must explain to the masses the impossibility of anything resembling a democratic peace, unless there are a series of revolutions and unless a revolutionary struggle is waged in every country against the *respective* government. Instead of allowing the bourgeois politicians to deceive the peoples with talk about the freedom of nations, socialists must explain to the masses in the *oppressor* nations that they cannot hope for their liberation, as long as they help oppress other nations, and do not recognise and uphold the right of those nations to self-determination, i.e., the freedom to secede. That is the socialist, as distinct from the imperialist, policy to be applied to all countries, on the question of peace and the national question. True, this line is in most cases incompatible with the laws punishing high treason—but so is the Basle resolution, which has been so shamefully betrayed by almost all the socialists of the oppressor nations.

The choice is between socialism and submission to the laws of Joffre and Hindenburg, between revolutionary struggle and servility to imperialism. There is no middle course. The greatest harm is caused to the proletariat by the hypocritical (or obtuse) authors of the "middle-course" policy.

Lenin Collected Works, Vol. 21, pp. 290–294

Notebooks on Imperialism, Notebook "Nu"

Notebooks on Imperialism *contains materials gathered by Lenin for his book* Imperialism, the Highest Stage of Capitalism. *The* Notebooks *were first published in a separate volume in 1939.*

Lenin Collected Works, Vol. 39

Chapter V. "Bismarck's Social Policy."

Being a country of "schools and barracks", Prussia naturally became a model of "imperialist social policy" (36): Bismarck's campaign against free thought, his flirting with the workers, universal suffrage (to set the bourgeoisie and the proletariat at loggerheads), social legislation... social insurance (Adler extols it).

In conclusion (p. 43), Adler says that this "must not" (!!ha-ha!!) be compared with the Caesarism of declining Rome, for support is given to people who work, not to good-for-nothing plebeians. *Proudhon*, he says, wrote (where?) (a quotation from *P r o u d h o n*: "We do not receive a penny from abroad", p. 43) that (Roman) Caesarism lived by plundering foreign nations, but this does not apply here.

‖ !!

... "Imperial-socialism ... in its enduring traits ... was, objectively, a great step forward towards integrating the proletariat in modern society and its practical collaboration in the latter's cultural tasks" (44). ((The roots of social-chauvinism!!))—hence "imperial-socialism" was "an illusion of world-historical importance", for it was useful, although it did not reconcile the proletariat, the enemy of Disraeli, Napoleon III and Bismarck.

Cf. Engels
on
Napoleon III
versus
Bismarck

"Bonapartism"

((End of Adler's pamphlet)).

SIEGFRIED, *NEW ZEALAND*

André Siegfried, *New Zealand*, Berlin, 1909.

(**N.B.** Chapter 28: "Imperialism.")

A very useful outline of a *broad* economic and political scope. The distinctive feature of "imperialism": exclusiveness. *T h e   y e l l o w   r a c e   i s   c o m- p l e t e l y   b a r r e d   f r o m   e n t e r i n g   t h e c o u n t r y.* **Savage** restrictions [e.g., £100!!!— p. 190] on immigration in general. A country at the edge of the world (*four* days to Australia!). Almost

‖ N.B.

103

as big as Italy, but with a population of less than one million!!! (*900,000*—p. 189; 929,000 in 1907, p. 234; half of France) ((magnificent climate, etc.)).

"Snobbishness" of the population (Chapter XXI): servility towards the aristocracy ("Sir" is a title of honour, before which they crawl), the British monarchy, the Court, etc., etc. Population growth is *very low*.

A country of inveterate, backwoods, thick-headed, egotistic philistines, who have brought their "**civilisation**" with them from England and keep it to themselves like a dog in the manger. (Exterminated the natives—the Maoris—by fire and sword; a series of wars.)

Example: persecution of the *A u s t r i a n* (N.B.) workers who emigrated to New Zealand (1893, 1898-) (p. 191): the "Labour Party" attacked them.

Equal rights for women.—Campaign against alcoholism.—Clericalism: intense religiosity; numerous sects.

Opposed to union with Australia: we are for ourselves. We are "the best country in, the world" (293) (!!)....

N.B. "New Zealand imperialism" (p. 294).... Its "special form" (ibidem) ... "colonial jingoism" (295 idem 296), which might be described as "Australasian imperialism" (295).

Two trends of imperialism (fully compatible):
1) Great-Power imperialism (participation in the imperialism of Great Britain). N.B.
N.B. "*local imperialism*" 2) **Local imperialism** (295)—its isolationism ... exclusiveness. N.B.

Protests against the French presence in New Caledonia—against the German occupation of Samoa (297), etc. This leads to irreconcilable hostility because of the "Greater New Zealand" idea....

In June 1901 New Zealand annexed the Cook Archipelago.

New Zealand is Great Britain's most "faithful", loyal colony.

The national debt: £ 51,200,000 (out of £ 66,500,000)—British capital Trade—66 per cent with Britain	Arch-patriots in the Boer war (307) ...(sent troops against the Boers)....

Prime Minister Seddon—a representative of Australasian imperialism. "An imperialist of the first water" (310) ... (he died June 10, 1906. Was Prime Minister (1893-1906) (p. 71))

His first trip to Britain—1897
 " second " " " —1902

"The champion of *s o c i a l p o l i c y* in him [Seddon] began to yield pride of place to the *i m p e r i a l i s t* and *protectionist* statesman" (311). Although a reformer (favoured reforms in New Zealand)—in Britain he made up to the *Tories*. The Conservatives lavished praise on the "socialist Seddon" (311). *T h e T i m e s*, June 18, 1902, praised Seddon, the radical, the democrat, the imperialist!! (quotation p. 311).

> N.B.
> social
> policy
> + imperialism!
>
> N.B.

Growth of the idea and practice of preferential tariffs....

Their "socialism": "The New Zealanders are practical and opportunist to the point of cynicism" (67)———and the workers too (67), they are wholly "conservative", they have something to "guard" (ibidem).

> N.B.

(Seddon—a representative of the "labour group in the Liberal Party" (68)).

Labour protection legislation—factory inspection—and of work in the home— a 48-hour working week (law of 1901) for men, 45 hours for women—minimum wage, etc.

Compulsory arbitration, etc.

The "key to all this is protectionism (140) and industrial *p r o s p e r i t y*.... ((It could not be maintained under free trade).... Old-age pensions (at 65)....

> N.B.:‖
> the
> imperialist
> bourgeoisie
> is buying the
> workers by
> social
> reforms

Creation of **small** landownership; large estates (stolen, etc., in the basest fashion from the Maoris, etc.) bought out and sold to smallholders—that is "*democracy*, but not *socialism*" (175). ((True!))

"Converting big landownership into small! That is what the French revolution did, too" (175)....

Imperialism, the Highest Stage of Capitalism

Written January–June 1916. First published in mid-1917 in pamphlet form.

Preface to the French and German Editions

… A few words must be said about Chapter VIII, "Parasitism and Decay of Capitalism." As already pointed out in the text, Hilferding, ex-"Marxist", and now a comrade-in-arms of Kautsky and one of the chief exponents of bourgeois, reformist policy in the Independent Social-Democratic Party of Germany, has taken a step backward on this question compared with the *frankly* pacifist and reformist Englishman, Hobson. The international split of the entire working-class movement is now quite evident (the Second and the Third Internationals). The fact that armed struggle and civil war is now raging between the two trends is also evident— the support given to Kolchak and Denikin in Russia by the Mensheviks and Socialist-Revolutionaries against the Bolsheviks; the fight the Scheidemanns and Noskes have conducted in conjunction with the

What is the economic basis of this world historical phenomenon? … It is precisely the parasitism and decay of capitalism, characteristic of its highest historical stage of development, i.e., imperialism.

[C]apitalism has now singled out a handful (less than one-tenth of the inhabitants of the globe; less than one-fifth at a most "generous" and liberal calculation) of exceptionally rich and powerful states which plunder the whole world simply by "clipping coupons."

bourgeoisie against the Spartacists in Germany; the same thing in Finland, Poland, Hungary, etc. What is the economic basis of this world historical phenomenon?

It is precisely the parasitism and decay of capitalism, characteristic of its highest historical stage of development, i.e., imperialism. As this pamphlet shows, capitalism has now singled out a *handful* (less than one-tenth of the inhabitants of the globe; less than one-fifth at a most "generous" and liberal calculation) of exceptionally rich and powerful states which plunder the whole world simply by "clipping coupons." Capital exports yield an income of eight to ten thousand million francs per annum, at pre-war prices and according to pre-war bourgeois statistics. Now, of course, they yield much more.

Obviously, out of such enormous *superprofits* (since they are obtained over and above the profits which capitalists squeeze out of the workers of their "own" country) it is *possible to bribe* the labour leaders and the upper stratum of the labour aristocracy. And that is just what the capitalists of the "advanced" countries are doing: they are bribing them in a thousand different ways, direct and indirect, overt and covert.

This stratum of workers-turned-bourgeois, or the labour aristocracy, who are quite philistine in their mode of life, in the size of their earnings and in their entire outlook, is the principal prop of the Second International, and in our days, the principal *social* (not military) *prop of the bourgeoisie*. For they are the real *agents of the bourgeoisie in the working-class* movement, the labour lieutenants of the capitalist class, real vehicles of reformism and chauvinism. In the civil war between the proletariat and the bourgeoisie they inevitably, and in no small numbers, take the side of the bourgeoisie, the "Versaillais" against the "Communards."

Unless the economic roots of this phenomenon are understood and its political and social significance is appreciated, not a step can be taken toward the solution of the practical problems of the communist movement and of the impending social revolution.

Imperialism is the eve of the social revolution of the proletariat. This has been confirmed since 1917 on a world-wide scale.

N. Lenin
July 6, 1920

Lenin Collected Works, Vol. 22, pp. 193–194

VI. Division of the World Among the Great Powers

... And Cecil Rhodes, we are informed by his intimate friend, the journalist Stead, expressed his imperialist views to him in 1895 in the following terms: "I was in the East End of London (a working-class quarter) yesterday and attended a meeting of the unemployed. I listened to the wild speeches, which were just a cry for 'bread! bread!' and on my way home I wondered over the scene and I became more than ever convinced of the importance of imperialism. ... My cherished idea is a solution for the social problem, i.e., in order to save the 40,000,000 inhabitants of the United Kingdom from a bloody civil war, we colonial statesmen must acquire new lands to settle the surplus population, to provide new markets for the goods produced in the factories and mines. The Empire, as I have always said, is a bread and butter question. If you want to avoid civil war, you must become imperialists."

That was said in 1895 by Cecil Rhodes, millionaire, a king of finance, the man who was mainly responsible for the Anglo–Boer War. True, his defence of imperialism is crude and cynical, but in substance it does not differ from the "theory" advocated by Messrs. Maslov, Südekum, Potresov, David, the founder of Russian Marxism and others. Cecil Rhodes was a somewhat more honest social-chauvinist. ...

Lenin Collected Works, Vol. 22, pp. 256–257

VII. Imperialism, as a Special Stage of Capitalism

... If it were necessary to give the briefest possible definition of imperialism we should have to say that imperialism is the monopoly stage of capitalism. Such a definition would include what is most important, for, on the one hand, finance capital is the bank capital of a few very big monopolist banks, merged with the capital of the monopolist associations of industrialists; and, on the other hand, the division of the world is the transition from a colonial policy which has extended without hindrance to territories unseized by any capitalist power, to a colonial policy of monopolist possession of the territory of the world, which has been completely divided up.

But very brief definitions, although convenient, for they sum up the main points, are nevertheless inadequate, since we have to deduce from them some especially important features of the phenomenon that has to be defined. And so, without forgetting the conditional and relative value of all definitions in general, which can never embrace all the concatenations of a phenomenon in its full development, we must give a definition of imperialism that will include the following five of its basic features:

(1) the concentration of production and capital has developed to such a high stage that it has created monopolies which play a decisive role in economic life; (2) the merging of bank capital with industrial capital, and the creation, on the basis of this "finance capital," of a financial oligarchy; (3) the export of capital as distinguished from the export of commodities acquires exceptional importance; (4) the formation of international monopolist capitalist associations which share the world among themselves, and (5) the

110

territorial division of the whole world among the biggest capitalist powers is completed. Imperialism is capitalism at that stage of development at which the dominance of monopolies and finance capital is established; in which the export of capital has acquired pronounced importance; in which the division of the world among the international trusts has begun, in which the division of all territories of the globe among the biggest capitalist powers has been completed.

We shall see later that imperialism can and must be defined differently if we bear in mind not only the basic, purely economic concepts—to which the above definition is limited—but also the historical place of this stage of capitalism in relation to capitalism in general, or the relation between imperialism and the two main trends in the working-class movement. ...

Lenin Collected Works, Vol. 22, pp. 266–267

VIII. Parasitism and Decay of Capitalism

We now have to examine yet another significant aspect of imperialism to which most of the discussions on the subject usually attach insufficient importance. One of the shortcomings of the Marxist Hilferding is that on this point he has taken a step backward compared with the non-Marxist Hobson. I refer to parasitism, which is characteristic of imperialism.

As we have seen, the deepest economic foundation of imperialism is monopoly. This is capitalist monopoly, i.e., monopoly which has grown out of capitalism and which exists in the general environment of capitalism, commodity production and competition, in permanent and insoluble contradiction to this general environment. Nevertheless, like all monopoly, it inevitably engenders a tendency to stagnation and decay. Since monopoly prices are established, even temporarily, the motive cause of technical and, consequently, of all other progress disappears to a certain extent and, further, the economic possibility arises of deliberately retarding technical progress. For instance, in America, a certain Owens invented a machine which revolutionised the manufacture of bottles. The German bottle-manufacturing cartel purchased Owens's patent, but pigeon-holed it, refrained from utilising it. Certainly, monopoly under capitalism can never completely, and for a very long period of time, eliminate competition in the world market (and this, by the by, is one of the reasons why the theory of ultra-imperialism is so absurd). Certainly, the possibility of reducing the cost of production and increasing profits by introducing technical improvements operates in the direction of change. But the tendency to stagnation and decay, which is characteristic of monopoly, continues to operate, and in some branches of industry, in some countries, for certain periods of time, it gains the upper hand.

The monopoly ownership of very extensive, rich or well situated colonies, operates in the same direction.

Further, imperialism is an immense accumulation of money capital in a few countries, amounting, as we have seen, to 100,000–150,000 million francs in securities. Hence the extraordinary growth of a class, or rather, of a stratum of rentiers, i.e., people who live by "clipping coupons," who take no part in any enterprise whatever, whose profession is idleness. The export of capital, one of the most essential economic bases of imperialism, still more completely isolates the rentiers from production and sets the seal of parasitism on the whole country that lives by exploiting the labour of several overseas countries and colonies.

"In 1893," writes Hobson, "the British capital invested abroad represented about 15 per cent of the total wealth of the United Kingdom." Let me remind the reader that by 1915 this capital had increased about two and a half times. "Aggressive imperialism," says Hobson further on, "which costs the tax-payer so dear, which is so little value to the manufacturer and trader ... is a source of great gain to the investor. ... The annual income Great Britain derives from commissions in her whole foreign and colonial trade, import and export, is estimated by Sir. R. Giffen at £18,000,000 (nearly 170 million rubles) for 1899, taken at 21 per cent, upon a turnover of £800,000,000." Great as this sum is, it cannot explain the aggressive imperialism of Great Britain, which is explained by the income of £90 million to £100 million from "invested" capital, the income of the rentiers.

The income of the rentiers is five *times* greater than the income obtained from the foreign trade of the biggest "trading" country in the world! This is the essence of imperialism and imperialist parasitism.

For that reason the term "rentier state" (*Rentner-staat*), or usurer state, is coming into common use in the economic literature that deals with imperialism. The world has become divided into a handful of usurer states and a vast majority of debtor states. "At the top of the list of foreign investments," says Schulze-Gaevernitz, "are those placed in politically dependent or allied countries: Great Britain grants loans to Egypt, Japan, China and South America. Her navy plays here the part of bailiff in case of necessity. Great Britain's political power protects her from the indignation of her debtors." Sartorius von Waltershausen in his book, *The National Economic System of Capital Investments Abroad*, cites Holland as the model "rentier state" and points out that Great Britain and France are now becoming such. Schilder is of the opinion that five industrial states have become "definitely pronounced creditor countries": Great Britain, France, Germany, Belgium and Switzerland. He does not include Holland in this list simply because she is "industrially little developed." The United States is a creditor only of the American countries.

"Great Britain," says Schulze-Gaevernitz, "is gradually becoming transformed from an industrial into a creditor state. Notwithstanding the absolute increase in industrial output and the export of manufactured goods, there is an increase in the relative importance of income from interest and dividends, issues of securities, commissions and speculation in the whole of the national economy. In my opinion it is precisely this that forms the economic basis of imperialist ascendancy. The creditor is more firmly attached to the debtor than the seller is to the buyer." In regard to Germany, A. Lansburgh, the publisher of the Berlin *Die Bank*, in 1911, in an article entitled "Germany—a Rentier State," wrote the following: "People in Germany are ready to sneer at the yearning to become rentiers that is observed in France. But they forget that as far as the bourgeoisie is concerned the situation in Germany is becoming more and more like that in France."

The rentier state is a state of parasitic, decaying capitalism, and this circumstance cannot fail to influence all the socio-political conditions of the countries concerned, in general, and the two fundamental trends in the working-class movement, in particular. To demonstrate this in the clearest possible manner let me quote Hobson, who is a most reliable witness, since he cannot be suspected of leaning towards Marxist orthodoxy; on the other hand, he is an Englishman who is very well acquainted with the situation in the country which is richest in colonies, in finance capital, and in imperialist experience.

With the Anglo–Boer War fresh in his mind, Hobson describes the connection between imperialism and the interests of the "financiers," their growing profits from contracts, supplies, etc., and writes: "While the directors of this definitely parasitic policy are capitalists, the same motives appeal to special classes of the workers. In many towns most important trades are dependent upon government employment or contracts; the imperialism of the metal and shipbuilding centres is attributable in no small degree to this fact."

...

The author is quite right: if the forces of imperialism had not been counteracted they would have led precisely to what he has described. The significance of a "United States of Europe" in the present imperialist situation is correctly appraised. He should have added, however, that, also *within* the working-class movement, the opportunists, who are for the moment victorious in most countries, are "working" systematically and undeviatingly in this very direction. Imperialism, which means the partitioning of the world, and the exploitation of other countries besides China, which means high monopoly profits for a handful of very rich countries, makes it economically possible to bribe the upper strata of the proletariat, and thereby fosters, gives shape to, and strengthens opportunism. We must not, however, lose sight of the forces which counteract imperialism in general, and opportunism in particular, and which, naturally, the social-liberal Hobson

Imperialism, which means the partitioning of the world, and the exploitation of other countries besides China, which means high monopoly profits for a handful of very rich countries, makes it economically possible to bribe the upper strata of the proletariat, and thereby fosters, gives shape to, and strengthens opportunism.

is unable to perceive.

The German opportunist, Gerhard Hildebrand, who was once expelled from the Party for defending imperialism, and who could today be a leader of the so-called "Social-Democratic" Party of Germany, supplements Hobson well by his advocacy of a "United States of Western Europe" (without Russia) for the purpose of "joint" action ... against the African Negroes, against the "great Islamic movement," for the maintenance of a "powerful army and navy," against a "Sino-Japanese coalition," etc.

The description of "British imperialism" in Schulze-Gaevernitz's book reveals the same parasitical traits. The national income of Great Britain approximately doubled from 1865 to 1898, while the income "from abroad" increased *ninefold* in the same period. While the "merit" of imperialism is that it "trains the Negro to habits of industry" (you cannot manage without coercion ...), the "danger" of imperialism lies in that "Europe will shift the burden of physical toil—first agricultural and mining, then the rougher work in industry—on to the coloured races, and itself be content with the role of rentier, and in this way, perhaps, pave the way for the economic, and later, the political emancipation of the coloured races."

An increasing proportion of land in England is being taken out of cultivation and used for sport, for the diversion of the rich. As far as Scotland—the most aristocratic place for hunting and other sports—is concerned, it is said that "it lives on its past and on Mr. Carnegie" (the American multimillionaire). On horse racing and fox hunting alone England annually spends £14,000,000 (nearly 130 million rubles). The number of rentiers in England is about one million. The percentage of the productively employed population to the total population is declining:

	Population England and Wales	Workers in basic industries	Per cent of total population
	(Millions)		
1851	17.9	4.1	23
1901	32.5	4.9	15

And in speaking of the British working class the bourgeois student of "British imperialism at the beginning of the twentieth century" is obliged to distinguish systematically between the *"upper stratum"* of the workers and the *"lower stratum of the proletariat proper."* The upper stratum furnishes the bulk of the membership of cooperatives, of trade unions, of sporting clubs and of numerous religious sects. To this level is adapted the electoral system, which in Great Britain is still *"sufficiently restricted to exclude the lower stratum of the proletariat proper"*! In order to present the condition of the British working class in a rosy light, only this upper stratum—which constitutes a *minority of* the proletariat—is usually spoken of. For instance, "the problem of unemployment is mainly a London problem and that of the lower proletarian stratum, *to which the politicians attach little importance* ..." He should have said: to which the bourgeois politicians and the "socialist" opportunists attach little importance.

One of the special features of imperialism connected with the facts I am describing, is the decline in emigration from imperialist countries and the increase in immigration into these countries from the more backward countries where lower wages are paid. As Hobson observes, emigration from Great Britain has been declining since 1884. In that year the number of emigrants was 242,000, while in 1900, the number was 169,000. Emigration from Germany reached the highest point between 1881 and 1890, with a total of 1,453,000 emigrants. In the course of the following two decades, it fell to 544,000 and to 341,000. On the other hand, there was an increase in the number of workers entering Germany from Austria, Italy, Russia and other countries. According to the 1907 census, there were 1,342,294 foreigners in Germany, of whom 440,800 were industrial workers and 257,329 agricultural workers. In France, the workers employed in the mining industry are, "in great part," foreigners: Poles, Italians and Spaniards. In the United States, immigrants from Eastern and Southern Europe are engaged in the most poorly paid jobs, while American workers provide the highest percentage of overseers or of the better-paid workers. Imperialism has the tendency to create privileged sections also among the workers, and to detach them from the broad masses of the proletariat.

It must be observed that in Great Britain the tendency of imperialism to split the workers, to strengthen opportunism among them and to cause temporary decay in the working-class movement, revealed itself much earlier than the end of the nineteenth and the beginning of the twentieth centuries; for two important distinguishing features of imperialism were already observed in Great Britain in the middle of the nineteenth century—vast colonial possessions and a monopolist position in the world market. Marx and Engels traced this connection between opportunism in the working-class movement and the imperialist features of British capitalism systematically, during the course of several decades. For example, on October 7, 1858, Engels wrote to Marx: "The English proletariat is actually becoming more and more bourgeois, so that this most bourgeois of all nations is apparently aiming ultimately at the possession of a bourgeois aristocracy and a bourgeois proletariat *alongside* the bourgeoisie. For a nation which exploits the whole world this is of course to a certain extent justifiable." Almost a quarter of a century later, in a letter dated August 11, 1881, Engels speaks of the "worst English trade unions which allow themselves to be led by men sold to, or at least paid by, the middle class." In a letter to Kautsky, dated September 12, 1882, Engels wrote: "You ask me what the English workers think about colonial policy. Well, exactly the same as they think about politics in general. There is no workers' party here, there are only Conservatives and Liberal-Radicals, and the workers gaily share the feast of England's monopoly of the world market and the colonies." (Engels expressed similar ideas in the press in his preface to the second edition of *The Condition of the Working Class in England*, which appeared in 1892.)

This clearly shows the causes and effects. The causes are: (1) exploitation of the whole world by this country; (2) its monopolist position in the world market, (3) its colonial monopoly. The effects are: (1) a section of the British proletariat becomes bourgeois; (2) a section of the proletariat allows itself to be led by men bought by, or at least paid by, the bourgeoisie. The imperialism of the beginning of the twentieth century completed the division of the world among a handful of states, each of which today exploits (in the sense of drawing superprofits from) a part of the "whole world" only a little smaller than that which England exploited in 1858; each of them occupies a monopolist position in the world market thanks to trusts, cartels, finance capital and creditor and debtor relations; each of them enjoys to some degree a colonial monopoly (we have seen that out of the total of *75,000,000* sq. km, which comprise the *whole* colonial world, *65,000,000* sq. km, or 86 per cent, belong to six powers; *61,000,000* sq. km, or 81 per cent, belong to three powers).

The distinctive feature of the present situation is the prevalence of such economic and political conditions that are bound to increase the irreconcilability between opportunism and the general and vital interests of the working-class movement: imperialism has grown from an embryo into the predominant system; capitalist monopolies occupy first place in economics and politics; the division of the world has been completed; on the other hand, instead of the undivided monopoly of Great Britain, we see a few imperialist powers contending for the right to share in this monopoly, and this struggle is characteristic of the whole period of the early twentieth century. Opportunism cannot now be completely triumphant in the working-class movement of one country for decades as it was in Britain in the second half of the nineteenth century; but in a number of countries it has grown ripe, overripe, and rotten, and has become completely merged with bourgeois policy in the form of "social-chauvinism."

Lenin Collected Works, Vol. 22, pp. 276–285

IX. Critique of Imperialism

By the critique of imperialism, in the broad sense of the term, we mean the attitude of the different classes of society towards imperialist policy in connection with their general ideology.

The enormous dimensions of finance capital concentrated in a few hands and creating an extraordinarily dense and widespread network of relationships and connections which subordinates not only the small and medium, but also the very small capitalists and small masters, on the one hand, and the increasingly intense struggle waged against other national state groups of financiers for the division of the world and domination over other countries, on the other hand, cause the propertied classes to go over entirely to the side of imperialism. "General" enthusiasm over the prospects of imperialism, furious defence of it and painting it in the brightest colours—such are the signs of the times. Imperialist ideology also penetrates the working class. No Chinese Wall separates it from the other classes. The leaders of the present-day, so-called, "Social-Democratic" Party of Germany are justly called "social-imperialists," that is, socialists in words and imperialists in deeds; but as early as 1902, Hobson noted the existence in Britain of "Fabian imperialists" who belonged to the opportunist Fabian Society.

Bourgeois scholars and publicists usually come out in defence of imperialism in a somewhat veiled form; they obscure its complete domination and its deep going roots, strive to push specific and secondary details into the forefront and do their very best to distract attention from essentials by means of absolutely ridiculous schemes

Imperialist ideology also penetrates the working class. No Chinese Wall separates it from the other classes. The leaders of the present-day, so-called, "Social-Democratic" Party of Germany are justly called "social-imperialists," that is, socialists in words and imperialists in deeds; but as early as 1902, Hobson noted the existence in Britain of "Fabian imperialists" who belonged to the opportunist Fabian Society.

for "reform," such as police supervision of the trusts or banks, etc. Cynical and frank imperialists who are bold enough to admit the absurdity of the idea of reforming the fundamental characteristics of imperialism are a rarer phenomenon.

…

The questions as to whether it is possible to reform the basis of imperialism, whether to go forward to the further intensification and deepening of the antagonisms which it engenders, or backward, towards allaying these antagonisms, are fundamental questions in the critique of imperialism. Since the specific political features of imperialism are reaction everywhere and increased national oppression due to the oppression of the financial oligarchy and the elimination of free competition, a petty-bourgeois-democratic opposition to imperialism arose at the beginning of the twentieth century in nearly all imperialist countries. Kautsky not only did not trouble to oppose, was not only unable to oppose this petty-bourgeois reformist opposition, which is really reactionary in its economic basis, but became merged with it in practice, and this is precisely where Kautsky and the broad international Kautskian trend deserted Marxism.

In the United States, the imperialist war waged against Spain in 1898 stirred up the opposition of the "anti-imperialists," the last of the Mohicans of bourgeois democracy, who declared this war to be "criminal," regarded the annexation of foreign territories as a violation of the Constitution, declared that the treatment of Aguinaldo, leader of the Filipinos (the Americans promised him the independence of his country, but later landed troops and annexed it), was "Jingo treachery," and quoted the words of Lincoln: "When the white man governs himself, that is self-government; but when he governs himself and also governs others, it is no longer self-government; it is despotism." But as long as all this criticism shrank from recognising the inseverable bond between imperialism and the trusts, and, therefore, between imperialism and the foundations of capitalism, while it shrank from joining the forces engendered by large-scale capitalism and its development—it remained a "pious wish."

Lenin Collected Works, Vol. 22, pp. 285–287

X. The Place of Imperialism in History

We have seen that in its economic essence imperialism is monopoly capitalism. This in itself determines its place in history, for monopoly that grows out of the soil of free competition, and precisely out of free competition, is the transition from the capitalist system to a higher socio-economic order. We must take special note of the four principal types of monopoly, or principal manifestations of monopoly capitalism, which are characteristic of the epoch we are examining.

Firstly, monopoly arose out of the concentration of production at a very high stage. This refers to the monopolist capitalist associations, cartels, syndicates and trusts. We have seen the important part these play in present-day economic life. At the beginning of the twentieth century, monopolies had acquired complete supremacy in the advanced countries, and although the first steps towards the formation of the cartels were taken by countries enjoying the protection of high tariffs (Germany, America), Great Britain, with her system of free trade, revealed the same basic phenomenon, only a little later, namely, the birth of monopoly out of the concentration of production.

Secondly, monopolies have stimulated the seizure of the most important sources of raw materials, especially for the basic and most highly cartelised industries in capitalist society: the coal and iron industries. The monopoly of the most important sources of raw materials has enormously increased the power of big capital, and has sharpened the antagonism between cartelised and non-cartelised industry.

125

Thirdly, monopoly has sprung from the banks. The banks have developed from modest middleman enterprise into the monopolists of finance capital. Some three to five of the biggest banks in each of the foremost capitalist countries have achieved the "personal link-up" between industrial and bank capital, and have concentrated in their hands the control of thousands upon thousands of millions which form the greater part of the capital and income of entire countries. A financial oligarchy, which throws a close network of dependence relationships over all the economic and political institutions of present-day bourgeois society without exception—such is the most striking manifestation of this monopoly.

Fourthly, monopoly has grown out of colonial policy. To the numerous "old" motives of colonial policy, finance capital has added the struggle for the sources of raw materials, for the export of capital, for spheres of influence, i.e., for spheres for profitable deals, concessions, monopoly profits and so on, economic territory in general. When the colonies of the European powers, for instance, comprised only one-tenth of the territory of Africa (as was the case in 1876), colonial policy was able to develop by methods other than those of monopoly—by the "free grabbing" of territories, so to speak. But when nine-tenths of Africa had been seized (by 1900), when the whole world had been divided up, there was inevitably ushered in the era of monopoly possession of colonies and, consequently, of particularly intense struggle for the division and the redivision of the world.

The extent to which monopolist capital has intensified all the contradictions of capitalism is generally known. It is sufficient to mention the high cost of living and the tyranny of the cartels.

This intensification of contradictions constitutes the most powerful driving force of the transitional period of history, which began from the time of the final victory of world finance capital.

Monopolies, oligarchy, the striving for domination and not for freedom, the exploitation of an increasing number of small or weak nations by a handful of the richest or most powerful nations—all these have given birth to those distinctive characteristics of imperialism which compel us to define it as parasitic or decaying capitalism. More and more prominently there emerges, as one of the tendencies of imperialism, the creation of the "rentier state," the usurer state, in which the bourgeoisie to an ever-increasing degree lives on the proceeds of capital exports and by "clipping coupons." It would be a mistake to believe that this tendency to decay precludes the rapid growth of capitalism. It does not. In the epoch of imperialism, certain branches of industry, certain strata of the bourgeoisie and certain countries betray, to a greater or lesser degree, now one and now another of these tendencies. On the whole, capitalism is growing far more rapidly than before; but this growth is not only becoming more and more uneven in general, its unevenness also manifests itself, in particular, in the decay of the countries which are richest in capital (Britain).

...

The receipt of high monopoly profits by the capitalists in one of the numerous branches of industry, in one of the numerous countries, etc., makes it economically possible for them to bribe certain sections of the workers, and for a time a fairly considerable minority of them, and win them to the side of the bourgeoisie of a given industry or given nation against all the others. The intensification

Monopolies, oligarchy, the striving for domination and not for freedom, the exploitation of an increasing number of small or weak nations by a handful of the richest or most powerful nations—all these have given birth to those distinctive characteristics of imperialism which compel us to define it as parasitic or decaying capitalism.

of antagonisms between imperialist nations for the division of the world increases this urge. And so there is created that bond between imperialism and opportunism, which revealed itself first and most clearly in Great Britain, owing to the fact that certain features of imperialist development were observable there much earlier than in other countries. Some writers, L. Martov, for example, are prone to wave aside the connection between imperialism and opportunism in the working-class movement—a particularly glaring fact at the present time—by resorting to "official optimism" (*à la* Kautsky and Huysmans) like the following: the cause of the opponents of capitalism would be hopeless if it were progressive capitalism that led to the increase of opportunism, or, if it were the best-paid workers who were inclined towards opportunism, etc. We must have no illusions about "optimism" of this kind. It is optimism in respect of opportunism; it is optimism which serves to conceal opportunism. As a matter of fact the extraordinary rapidity and the particularly revolting character of the development of opportunism is by no means a guarantee that its victory will be durable: the rapid growth of a painful abscess on a healthy body can only cause it to burst more quickly and thus relieve the body of it. The most dangerous of all in this respect are those who do not wish to understand that the fight against imperialism is a sham and humbug unless it is inseparably bound up with the fight against opportunism. ...

Lenin Collected Works, Vol. 22, pp. 298–302

A Caricature of Marxism and Imperialist Economism

Written August–October 1916. First published in the magazine Zvezda *No. 1 and 2, 1924.*

5. "Monism and Dualism"

… Is the *actual* condition of the workers in the oppressor and in the oppressed nations the same, from the standpoint of the national question?

No, it is not the same.

(1) *Economically*, the difference is that sections of the working class in the oppressor nations receive crumbs from the *superprofits* the bourgeoisie of these nations obtains by extra exploitation of the workers of the oppressed nations. Besides, economic statistics show that here a *larger* percentage of the workers become "straw bosses" than is the case in the oppressed nations, a larger percentage rise to the labour *aristocracy*. That is a fact. To a *certain degree* the workers of the oppressor nations are partners of *their own* bourgeoisie in plundering the workers (and the **To a certain degree the workers of the oppressor nations are partners of their own bourgeoisie in plundering the workers (and the mass of the population) of the oppressed nations.**

mass of the population) of the oppressed nations.

(2) *Politically*, the difference is that, compared with the workers of the oppressed nations, they occupy a *privileged* position in many spheres of political life.

(3) *Ideologically*, or spiritually, the difference is that they are taught, at school and in life, disdain and contempt for the workers of the oppressed nations. This has been *experienced*, for example, by every Great Russian who has been brought up or who has lived among Great Russians.

Thus, *all along the line* there are differences in objective reality, i.e., "dualism" in the objective world that is independent of the will and consciousness of individuals.

That being so, how are we to regard P. Kievsky's assertion about the "monistic action of the International"?

It is a hollow, high-sounding phrase, no more:

In *real life* the International is composed of workers *divided* into oppressor and oppressed nations. *If* its action is *to be monistic*, its propaganda must *not* be the same for both. That is how we should regard the matter in the light of real (not Dühringian) "monism," Marxist materialism.

    …

5) *Why* must "we" "actively resist" suppression of a national uprising? P. Kievsky advances only one reason: "… we shall thereby be combating imperialism, our mortal enemy." All the *strength* of this argument lies in the *strong* word "mortal." And this is in keeping with his penchant for strong words instead of strong arguments— high-sounding phrases like "driving a stake into the quivering body of the bourgeoisie" and similar Alexinsky flourishes.

But this Kievsky argument is *wrong*. Imperialism is as much our "mortal" enemy as is capitalism. That is so. No Marxist will forget, however, that capitalism is progressive compared with feudalism, and that imperialism is progressive compared with pre-monopoly capitalism. Hence, it is *not* every struggle against imperialism that we should support. We will *not* support a struggle of the reactionary classes against imperialism; we will *not* support an uprising of the reactionary classes against imperialism and capitalism.

Consequently, once the author admits the need to support an uprising of an oppressed nation ("actively resisting" suppression means supporting the uprising), he also admits that a national uprising is *progressive*, that the establishment of a separate and new state, of new frontiers, etc., resulting from a successful uprising, is *progressive*.

Lenin Collected Works, Vol. 23, pp. 55–56, 63

Imperialism and the Split in Socialism (Full text)

Written in October 1916. First published in Sbornik Sotsial-Demokrata *No. 2, December 1916.*

Is there any connection between imperialism and the monstrous and disgusting victory opportunism (in the form of social-chauvinism) has gained over the labour movement in Europe?

This is the fundamental question of modern socialism. And having in our Party literature fully established, first, the imperialist character of our era and of the present war, and, second, the inseparable historical connection between social-chauvinism and opportunism, as well as the intrinsic similarity of their political ideology, we can and must proceed to analyse this fundamental question.

We have to begin with as precise and full a definition of imperialism as possible. Imperialism is a specific historical stage of capitalism. Its specific character is three-fold: imperialism is (1) monopoly capitalism; (2) parasitic, or decaying capitalism; (3) moribund capitalism. The supplanting of free competition by monopoly is the fundamental economic feature, the *quintessence* of imperialism. Monopoly manifests itself in five principal forms: (1) cartels, syndicates and trusts—the concentration of production has reached a degree which gives rise to these monopolistic associations of capitalists; (2) the monopolistic position of the big banks—three, four or five giant banks manipulate the whole economic life of America, France, Germany; (3) seizure of the sources of *raw material* by the trusts and the financial oligarchy (finance capital

133

is monopoly industrial capital merged with bank capital); (4) the (economic) partition of the world by the international cartels has *begun*. There are already over *one hundred* such international cartels, which command the *entire* world market and divide it "amicably" among themselves—until war *re*divides it. The export of capital, as distinct from the export of commodities under non-monopoly capitalism, is a highly characteristic phenomenon and is closely linked with the economic and territorial-political partition of the world; (5) the territorial partition of the world (colonies) is *completed*.

Imperialism, as the highest stage of capitalism in America and Europe, and later in Asia, took final shape in the period 1898–1914. The Spanish–American War (1898), the Anglo–Boer War (1899–1902), the Russo–Japanese War (1904–05) and the economic crisis in Europe in 1900 are the chief historical landmarks in the new era of world history.

The fact that imperialism is parasitic or decaying capitalism is manifested first of all in the tendency to decay, which is characteristic of *every* monopoly under the system of private ownership of the means of production. The difference between the democratic-republican and the reactionary-monarchist imperialist bourgeoisie is obliterated precisely because they are both rotting alive (which by no means precludes an extraordinarily rapid development of capitalism in individual branches of industry, in individual countries, and in individual periods). Secondly, the decay of capitalism is manifested in the creation of a huge stratum of rentiers, capitalists who live by "clipping coupons." In each of the four leading imperialist countries—England, U.S.A., France and Germany—capital in securities amounts to 100,000 or 150,000 *million* francs, from which each country derives an annual income of no less than five to eight thousand million. Thirdly, export of capital is parasitism raised to a high pitch. Fourthly, "finance capital strives for domination, not freedom." Political reaction *all along* the line is a characteristic feature of imperialism. Corruption, bribery on a huge scale and all kinds of fraud. Fifthly, the exploitation of oppressed nations—which is inseparably connected with annexations—and especially the exploitation of colonies by a handful of "Great" Powers, increasingly transforms the "civilised" world into a parasite on the body of hundreds of millions in the uncivilised nations. The Roman proletarian lived at the expense of society. Modern society lives at the expense of the modern proletarian. Marx specially stressed this profound observation of Sismondi. Imperialism somewhat changes the situation. A privileged upper stratum of the proletariat in the imperialist countries lives partly at the expense of hundreds of millions in the uncivilised nations.

It is clear why imperialism is *moribund* capitalism, capitalism in *transition* to socialism: monopoly, which grows *out of* capitalism, is *already* dying capitalism, the beginning of its transition to socialism. The tremendous *socialization* of labour by imperialism (what its apologists—the bourgeois economists—call "interlocking") produces the same result.

Advancing this definition of imperialism brings us into complete contradiction to K. Kautsky, who refuses to regard imperialism as a "phase of capitalism" and defines it as a *policy* "preferred" by finance capital, a tendency of "industrial" countries to annex "agrarian" countries. Kautsky's definition is thoroughly false from the theoretical standpoint. What distinguishes imperialism is the rule *not* of industrial capital, but of finance capital, the striving to annex *not* agrarian countries, particularly, but *every* kind of country. Kautsky *divorces* imperialist politics from imperialist economics, he divorces monopoly in politics from monopoly in economics in order to pave the way for his vulgar bourgeois reformism, such as "disarmament," "ultra-imperialism" and similar nonsense. The whole purpose and significance of this theoretical falsity is to obscure the *most profound* contradictions of imperialism and thus justify the theory of "unity" with the apologists of imperialism, the outright social-chauvinists and opportunists.

We have dealt at sufficient length with Kautsky's break with Marxism on this point in *Sotsial-Demokrat* and *Kommunist*. Our Russian Kautskyites, the supporters of the Organising Committee (O.C.), headed by Axelrod and Spectator, including even Martov, and to a large degree Trotsky, preferred to maintain a discreet silence on the question of Kautskyism as a trend. They did not dare defend Kautsky's war-time writings, confining themselves simply to praising Kautsky (Axelrod in his German pamphlet, which the Organising Committee has *promised* to publish in Russian) or to quoting Kautsky's private letters (Spectator), in which he says he belongs to the opposition and jesuitically tries to nullify his chauvinist declarations.

It should be noted that Kautsky's "conception" of imperialism—which is tantamount to embellishing imperialism—is a retrogression not only compared with Hilferding's *Finance Capital* (no matter how assiduously Hilferding now defends Kautsky and "unity" with the social-chauvinists!) but also compared with the *social-liberal* J. A. Hobson. This English economist, who in no way claims to be a Marxist, defines imperialism, and reveals its contradictions, much more profoundly in a book published in 1902. This is what Hobson (in whose book may be found nearly all Kautsky's pacifist and "conciliatory" banalities) wrote on the highly important question of the parasitic nature of imperialism:

Two sets of circumstances, in Hobson's opinion, weakened the power of the old empires: (1) "economic parasitism," and (2) formation of armies from dependent peoples. "There is first the habit of economic parasitism, by which the ruling state has used its provinces, colonies, and dependencies in order to enrich its ruling class and to bribe its lower classes into acquiescence." Concerning the second circumstance, Hobson writes:

> One of the strangest symptoms of the blindness of imperialism [this song about the "blindness" of imperialists comes more appropriately from the social-liberal Hobson than from the "Marxist" Kautsky] is the reckless indifference with which Great Britain, France, and other imperial nations are embarking on this perilous dependence. Great Britain has gone farthest. Most of the fighting by which we have won our Indian Empire has been done by natives; in India, as more recently in Egypt, great standing armies are placed under British commanders; almost all the fighting associated with our African dominions, except in the southern part, has been done for us by natives.

The prospect of partitioning China elicited from Hobson the following economic appraisal: "The greater part of Western Europe might then assume the appearance and character already exhibited by tracts of country in the South of England, in the Riviera, and in the tourist-ridden or residential parts of Italy and Switzerland, little clusters of wealthy aristocrats drawing dividends and pensions from the Far East, with a somewhat larger group of professional retainers and tradesmen and a larger body of personal servants and workers in the transport trade and in the final stages of production of the more perishable goods: all the main arterial industries would have disappeared, the staple foods and semi-manufactures flowing in as tribute from Asia and Africa. ... We have foreshadowed the possibility of even a larger alliance of Western states, a European federation of Great Powers which, so far from forwarding the cause of world civilisation, might introduce the gigantic peril of a Western parasitism, a group of advanced industrial nations, whose upper classes drew vast tribute from Asia and Africa, with which they supported great tame masses of retainers, no longer engaged in the staple industries of agriculture and manufacture, but kept in the performance of personal or minor industrial services under the control of a new financial aristocracy. Let those who would scout such a theory [he should have said: prospect] as undeserving of consideration examine the economic and social condition of districts in Southern England today which are already reduced to this condition, and reflect upon the vast extension of such a system which might be rendered feasible by the subjection of China to the economic control of similar groups of financiers, investors [rentiers] and political and business officials, draining the greatest potential reservoir of profit the world has ever known, in order to consume it in Europe. The situation is far too complex, the play of world forces far too incalculable, to render this or any other single interpretation of the future very probable; but the influences which

[T]he opportunists (social-chauvinists) are working hand in glove with the imperialist bourgeoisie precisely towards creating an imperialist Europe on the backs of Asia and Africa ... objectively the opportunists are a section of the petty bourgeoisie and of certain strata of the working class who have been bribed out of imperialist super-profits and converted into watchdogs of capitalism and corruptors of the labour movement.

govern the imperialism of Western Europe today are moving in this direction, and, unless counteracted or diverted, make towards such a consummation."

Hobson, the social-liberal, fails to see that this "counteraction" can be offered *only* by the revolutionary proletariat and *only* in the form of a social revolution. But then he is a social-liberal! Nevertheless, as early as 1902 he had an excellent insight into the meaning and significance of a "United States of Europe" (be it said for the benefit of Trotsky the Kautskyite!) and of all that is now being glossed over by the *hypocritical Kautskyites* of various countries, namely, that the *opportunists*

139

(social-chauvinists) are working hand in glove with the imperialist bourgeoisie *precisely* towards creating an imperialist Europe on the backs of Asia and Africa, and that objectively the *opportunists* are a section of the petty bourgeoisie and of certain strata of the working class who *have been bribed* out of imperialist superprofits and converted into *watchdogs* of capitalism and *corruptors* of the labour movement.

Both in articles and in the resolutions of our Party, we have repeatedly pointed to this most profound connection, the economic connection, between the imperialist bourgeoisie and the opportunism which has triumphed (for long?) in the labour movement. And from this, incidentally, we concluded that a split with the social-chauvinists was inevitable. Our Kautskyites preferred to evade the question! Martov, for instance, uttered in his lectures a sophistry which in the *Bulletin of the Organising Committee, Secretariat Abroad* (No. 4, April 10, 1916) is expressed as follows:

> ... The cause of revolutionary Social-Democracy would be in
> a sad, indeed hopeless, plight if those groups of workers who
> in mental development approach most closely to the "intel-
> ligentsia" and who are the most highly skilled fatally drifted
> away from it towards opportunism. ...

By means of the silly word "fatally" and a certain sleight-of-hand, the *fact* is *evaded* that *certain* groups of workers *have already drifted away* to opportunism and to the imperialist bourgeoisie! And that is the very fact the sophists of the O.C. want to *evade*! They confine themselves to the "official optimism" the Kautskyite Hilferding and many others now flaunt: objective conditions guarantee the unity of the proletariat and the victory of the revolutionary trend! We, forsooth, are "optimists" with regard to the proletariat!

But in reality all these Kautskyites—Hilferding, the O.C. supporters, Martov and Co.—are *optimists* ... with regard to *opportunism*. That is the whole point!

The proletariat is the child of capitalism—of world capitalism, and not only of European capitalism, or of imperialist capitalism. On a world scale, fifty years sooner or fifty years later—measured on a *world* scale this is a minor point—the "proletariat" of course "will be" united, and revolutionary Social-Democracy will "inevitably" be victorious within it. But that is not the point, Messrs. Kautskyites. The point is that at the present time, in the imperialist countries of Europe, *you are fawning* on the opportunists, who are *alien* to the proletariat as a class, who are the servants, the agents of the bourgeoisie and the vehicles of its influence, and *unless* the labour movement *rids* itself of them, it will remain a *bourgeois labour movement.* By advocating "unity" with the opportunists, with the Legiens and Davids, the Plekhanovs, the Chkhenkelis and Potresovs, etc., you are, objectively, defending the *enslavement* of the workers by the imperialist bourgeoisie with the aid of its best agents in the labour movement. The victory of revolutionary Social-Democracy on a world scale is absolutely inevitable, only it is moving and will move, is proceeding and will proceed, *against* you, it will be a victory *over* you.

These two trends, one might even say *two* parties, in the present-day labour movement, which in 1914–16 so obviously parted ways all over the world, *were traced by Engels and Marx in England* throughout the course of *decades*, roughly from 1858 to 1892.

Neither Marx nor Engels lived to see the imperialist epoch of world capitalism, which began not earlier than 1898–1900. But it has been a peculiar feature of England that even in the middle of the nineteenth century she already revealed at least *two* major distinguishing features of imperialism: (1) vast colonies, and (2) monopoly profit (due to her monopoly position in the world market). In both respects England at that time was an exception among capitalist countries, and Engels and Marx, analysing this exception, quite clearly and definitely indicated its *connection* with the (temporary) victory of opportunism in the English labour movement.

In a letter to Marx, dated October 7, 1858, Engels wrote: "... The English proletariat is actually becoming more and more bourgeois, so that this most bourgeois of all nations is apparently aiming ultimately at the possession of a bourgeois aristocracy and a bourgeois proletariat *alongside* the bourgeoisie. For a nation which exploits the whole world this is of course to a certain extent justifiable." In a letter to Sorge, dated September 21, 1872, Engels informs him that Hales kicked up a big row in the Federal Council of the International and secured a vote of censure on Marx for saying that "the English labour leaders had sold themselves." Marx wrote to Sorge on August 4, 1874: "As to the urban workers here [in England], it is a pity that the whole pack of leaders did not get into Parliament. This would be the surest way of getting rid of the whole lot." In a letter to Marx, dated August 11, 1881, Engels speaks about "those very worst English trade unions which allow themselves to be led by men sold to, or at least paid by, the bourgeoisie." In a letter to Kautsky, dated September 12, 1882, Engels wrote: "You ask me what the English workers think about colonial policy. Well, exactly the same as they think about politics in general. There is no workers' party here, there are only Conservatives and Liberal-Radicals, and the workers gaily share the feast of England's monopoly of the world market and the colonies."

On December 7, 1889, Engels wrote to Sorge: "The most repulsive thing here [in England] is the bourgeois 'respectability', which has grown deep into the bones of the workers. ... Even Tom Mann, whom I regard as the best of the lot, is fond of mentioning that he will be lunching with the Lord Mayor. If one compares this with the French, one realises what a revolution is good for, after all." In a letter, dated April 19, 1890: "But *under* the surface the movement [of the working class in England] is going on, is embracing ever wider sections and mostly just among the hitherto stagnant *lowest* [Engels's italics] strata. The day is no longer far off when this mass *will* suddenly *find itself*, when it will dawn upon it that it itself is this colossal mass in motion." On March 4, 1891: "The failure of the collapsed Dockers' Union; the 'old' conservative trade unions, *rich* and therefore cowardly, remain lone on the field. ..." September 14, 1891: at the Newcastle Trade Union Congress the old unionists, opponents of the eight-hour day, were defeated "and the bourgeois papers recognise the defeat of the *bourgeois labour party*" (Engels's italics throughout) ...

That these ideas, which were repeated by Engels over the course of decades, were also expressed by him publicly, in the press, is proved by his preface to the second edition of *The Condition of the Working Class in England*, 1892. Here he speaks of an "aristocracy among the working class," of a "privileged minority of the workers," in contradistinction to the "great mass of working people." "A small, privileged, protected minority" of the working class alone was "permanently benefited" by the privileged position of England in 1848–68, whereas "the great bulk of them experienced at best but a temporary improvement." ... "With the break-down of that [England's industrial] monopoly, the English working class will loose that privileged position. ..." The members of the "new" unions, the unions of the unskilled workers, "had this immense advantage, that their minds were virgin soil, entirely free from the inherited 'respectable' bourgeois prejudices which hampered the brains of the better situated 'old unionists'." ... "The so-called workers' representatives" in England are people "who are forgiven their being members of the working class because they themselves would like to drown their quality of being workers in the ocean of their liberalism ..."

We have deliberately quoted the direct statements of Marx and Engels at rather great length in order that the reader may study them *as a whole*. And they should be studied, they are worth carefully pondering over. For they are the *pivot* of the tactics in the labour movement that are dictated by the objective conditions of the imperialist era.

Here, too, Kautsky has tried to "befog the issue" and substitute for Marxism sentimental conciliation with the opportunists. Arguing against the avowed and naive social-imperialists (men like Lensch) who justify Germany's participation in the war as a means of destroying England's monopoly, Kautsky *"corrects"* this obvious falsehood by another equally obvious falsehood. Instead of a cynical falsehood he employs a suave falsehood!

The *industrial* monopoly of England, he says, has long ago been broken, has long ago been destroyed, and there is nothing left to destroy.

Why is this argument false?

Because, firstly, it overlooks England's *colonial* monopoly. Yet Engels, as we have seen, pointed to this very clearly as early as 1882, thirty-four years ago! Although England's industrial monopoly may have been destroyed, her colonial monopoly not only remains, but has become extremely accentuated, for the whole world is already divided up! By means of this suave lie Kautsky smuggles in the bourgeois-pacifist and opportunist-philistine idea that "there is nothing to fight about." On the contrary not only have the *capitalists* something to fight about now, but they *cannot help* fighting if they want to preserve capitalism, for without a forcible redivision of colonies the *new* imperialist countries cannot obtain the privileges enjoyed by the older *(and weaker)* imperialist powers.

Secondly, why does England's monopoly explain the (temporary) victory of opportunism in England? Because monopoly yields *superprofits*, i.e., a surplus of profits over and above the capitalist profits that are normal and customary all over the world. The capitalists *can* devote a part (and not a small one, at that!) of these superprofits to bribe *their own* workers, to create something like an alliance (recall the celebrated "alliances" described by the Webbs of English trade unions and employers) between the workers of the given nation and their capitalists *against* the other countries. England's industrial monopoly was already destroyed by the end of the nineteenth century. That is beyond dispute. But *how* did this destruction take place? Did *all* monopoly disappear?

145

If that were so, Kautsky's "theory" of conciliation (with the opportunists) would to a certain extent be justified. But it is *not* so, and that is just the point. Imperialism *is* monopoly capitalism. Every cartel, trust, syndicate, every giant bank *is* a monopoly. Superprofits have not disappeared; they still remain. The exploitation of *all* other countries by one privileged, financially wealthy country remains and has become more intense. A handful of wealthy countries—there are only four of them, if we mean independent, really gigantic, "modern" wealth: England, France, the United States and Germany—have developed monopoly to vast proportions, they obtain *super*profits running into hundreds, if not thousands, of millions, they "ride on the backs" of hundreds and hundreds of millions of people in other countries and fight among themselves for the division of the particularly rich, particularly fat and particularly easy spoils.

This, in fact, is the economic and political essence of imperialism, the profound contradictions of which Kautsky glosses over instead of exposing.

The bourgeoisie of an imperialist "Great" Power *can economically* bribe the upper strata of "its" workers by spending on this a hundred million or so francs a year, for its *super*profits most likely amount to about a thousand million. And how this little sop is divided among the labour ministers, "labour representatives" (remember Engels's splendid analysis of the term), labour members of war industries committees, labour officials, workers belonging to the narrow craft unions, office employees, etc., etc., is a secondary question.

Between 1848 and 1868, and to a certain extent even later,

only England enjoyed a monopoly: *that is why* opportunism could prevail there for decades. *No* other countries possessed either very rich colonies or an industrial monopoly.

The last third of the nineteenth century saw the transition to the new, imperialist era. Finance capital *not* of one, but of several, though very few, Great Powers enjoys a monopoly. (In Japan and Russia the monopoly of military power, vast territories, or special facilities for robbing minority nationalities, China, etc., partly supplements, partly takes the place of, the monopoly of modern, up-to-date finance capital.) This difference explains why England's monopoly position *could* remain *unchallenged* for decades. The monopoly of modern finance capital is being frantically challenged; the era of imperialist wars has begun. It was possible in those days to bribe and corrupt the working class of *one* country for decades. This is now improbable, if not impossible. But on the other hand, *every* imperialist "Great" Power can and does bribe *smaller* strata (than in England in 1848–68) of the "labour aristocracy." Formerly a *"bourgeois labour party,"* to use Engels's remarkably profound expression, could arise only in one country, because it alone enjoyed a monopoly, but, on the other hand, it could exist for a long time. Now a *"bourgeois labour party" is inevitable* and typical in *all* imperialist countries; but in view of the desperate struggle they are waging for the division of spoils, it is improbable that such a party can prevail for long in a number of countries. For the trusts, the financial oligarchy, high prices, etc., while *enabling* the bribery of a handful in the top layers, are increasingly oppressing, crushing, ruining and torturing the *mass* of the proletariat and the semi-proletariat.

On the one hand, there is the tendency of the bourgeoisie and the opportunists to convert a handful of very rich and privileged nations into "eternal" parasites on the body of the rest of mankind, to "rest on the laurels" of the exploitation of Negroes, Indians, etc., keeping them in subjection with the aid of the excellent weapons of extermination provided by modern militarism. On the other hand, there is the tendency of the *masses*, who are more oppressed than before and who bear the whole brunt of imperialist wars, to cast off this yoke and to overthrow the bourgeoisie. It is in the struggle between these two tendencies that the history of the labour movement will now inevitably develop. For the first tendency is not accidental; it is "substantiated" economically. In *all* countries the bourgeoisie has already begotten, fostered and secured for itself "bourgeois labour parties" of social-chauvinists. The difference between a definitely formed party, like Bissolati's in Italy, for example, which is fully social-imperialist, and, say, the semi-formed near-party of the Potresovs, Gvozdyovs, Bulkins, Chkheidzes, Skobelevs and Co., is an immaterial difference. The important thing is that economically, the desertion of a stratum of the labour aristocracy to the bourgeoisie has matured and become an accomplished fact; and this economic fact, this shift in class relations, will find political form, in one shape or another, without any particular "difficulty."

On the economic basis referred to above, the political institutions of modern capitalism—press, parliament, associations, congresses, etc.—have created *political* privileges and sops for the respectful, meek, reformist and patriotic office employees and workers, corresponding to the economic privileges and sops.

Lucrative and soft jobs in the government or on the war industries committees, in parliament and on diverse committees, on the editorial staffs of "respectable," legally published newspapers or on the management councils of no less respectable and "bourgeois law-abiding" trade unions—this is the bait by which the imperialist bourgeoisie attracts and rewards the representatives and supporters of the "bourgeois labour parties."

The mechanics of political democracy works in the same direction. Nothing in our times can be done without elections; nothing can be done without the masses. And in this era of printing and parliamentarism it is *impossible* to gain the following of the masses without a widely ramified, systematically managed, well-equipped system of flattery, lies, fraud, juggling with fashionable and popular catchwords, and promising all manner of reforms and blessings to the workers right and left—as long as they renounce the revolutionary struggle for the overthrow of the bourgeoisie. I would call this system Lloyd-Georgism, after the English Minister Lloyd George, one of the foremost and most dexterous representatives of this system in the classic land of the "bourgeois labour party." A first-class bourgeois manipulator, an astute politician, a popular orator who will deliver any speeches you like, even r-r-revolutionary ones, to a labour audience, and a man who is capable of obtaining sizable sops for docile workers in the shape of social reforms (insurance, etc.), Lloyd George serves the bourgeoisie splendidly, and serves it precisely *among* the workers, brings its influence *precisely* to the proletariat, to where the bourgeoisie needs it most and where it finds it most difficult to subject the masses morally.

And is there such a great difference between Lloyd George

149

and the Scheidemanns, Legiens, Hendersons and Hyndmans, Plekhanovs, Renaudels and Co.? Of the latter, it may be objected, some will return to the revolutionary socialism of Marx. This is possible, but it is an insignificant difference in degree, if the question is regarded from its political, i.e., its mass aspect. Certain individuals among the present social-chauvinist leaders may return to the proletariat. But the social-chauvinist or (what is the same thing) opportunist *trend* can neither disappear nor "return" to the revolutionary proletariat. Wherever Marxism is popular among the workers, this political trend, this "bourgeois labour party," will swear by the name of Marx. It cannot be prohibited from doing this, just as a trading firm cannot be prohibited from using any particular label, sign or advertisement. It has always been the case in history that after the death of revolutionary leaders who were popular among the oppressed classes, their enemies have attempted to appropriate their names so as to deceive the oppressed classes.

The fact is that "bourgeois labour parties," as a political phenomenon, have already been formed in *all* the foremost capitalist countries, and that

> Certain individuals among the present social-chauvinist leaders may return to the proletariat. But the social-chauvinist or (what is the same thing) opportunist trend can neither disappear nor "return" to the revolutionary proletariat.

unless a determined and relentless struggle is waged all along the line against these parties—or groups, trends, etc., it is all the same—there can be no question of a struggle against imperialism, or of Marxism, or of a socialist labour movement. The Chkheidze faction, *Nashe Dyelo* and *Golos Truda* in Russia, and the O.C. supporters abroad are nothing but varieties of one *such* party. There is not the slightest reason for thinking that these parties will disappear *before* the social revolution. On the contrary, the nearer the revolution approaches, the more strongly it flares up and the more sudden and violent the transitions and leaps in its progress, the greater will be the part the struggle of the revolutionary mass stream against the opportunist petty-bourgeois stream will play in the labour movement. Kautskyism is not an independent trend, because it has no roots either in the masses or in the privileged stratum which has deserted to the bourgeoisie. But the danger of Kautskyism lies in the fact that, utilising the ideology of the past, it endeavours to reconcile the proletariat with the "bourgeois labour party," to preserve the unity of the proletariat with that party and thereby enhance the latter's prestige. The masses no longer follow the avowed social-chauvinists: Lloyd George has been hissed down at workers' meetings in England; Hyndman has left the party; the Renaudels and Scheidemanns, the Potresovs and Gvozdyovs are protected by the police. The Kautskyites' masked defence of the social-chauvinists is much more dangerous.

One of the most common sophistries of Kautskyism is its reference to the "masses." We do not want, they say, to break away from the masses and mass organisations! But just think how Engels put the question. In the nineteenth century the "mass organisations"

151

of the English trade unions were on the side of the bourgeois labour party. Marx and Engels did not reconcile themselves to it on this ground; they exposed it. They did not forget, firstly, that the trade union organisations directly embraced a *minority of the proletariat*. In England then, as in Germany now, not more than one-fifth of the proletariat was organised. No one can seriously think it possible to organise the majority of the proletariat under capitalism. Secondly—and this is the main point—it is not so much a question of the size of an organisation, as of the real, objective significance of its policy: does its policy represent the masses, does it serve them, i.e., does it aim at their liberation from capitalism, or does it represent the interests of the minority, the minority's reconciliation with capitalism? The latter was true of England in the nineteenth century, and it is true of Germany, etc., now.

Engels draws a distinction between the "bourgeois labour party" of the *old* trade unions—the privileged minority—and the *"lowest mass,"* the real majority, and appeals to the latter, who are not infected by "bourgeois respectability." This is the essence of Marxist tactics!

Neither we nor anyone else can calculate precisely what portion of the proletariat is following and will follow the social-chauvinists and opportunists. This will be revealed only by the struggle, it will be definitely decided only by the socialist revolution. But we know for certain that the "defenders of the fatherland" in the imperialist war *represent* only a minority. And it is therefore our duty, if we wish to remain socialists, to go down *lower and deeper*, to the real masses; this is the whole meaning and the whole purport of the struggle against opportunism. By exposing the fact that the opportunists and social-chauvinists are in reality betraying and selling the interests of the masses, that they are defending the temporary privileges of a minority of the workers, that they are the vehicles of bourgeois ideas and influences, that they are really allies and agents of the bourgeoisie, we teach the masses to appreciate their true political interests, to fight for socialism and for the revolution through all the long and painful vicissitudes of imperialist wars and imperialist armistices.

The only Marxist line in the world labour movement is to explain to the masses the inevitability and necessity of breaking with opportunism, to educate them for revolution by waging a relentless struggle against opportunism, to utilise the experiences of the war to expose, not conceal, the utter vileness of national-liberal labour politics.

In the next article, we shall try to sum up the principal features that distinguish this line from Kautskyism.

Lenin Collected Works, Vol. 23, pp. 105–120

Ten "Socialist" Ministers (Full text)

Published in Sotsial-Demokrat *No. 56, November 6, 1916.*

Huysmans, the Secretary of the International Social-Chauvinist Bureau, has sent a telegram of greetings to Danish Minister without portfolio Stauning, the leader of the Danish quasi-"Social-Democratic" Party. The telegram reads: "I learn from the newspapers that you have been appointed Minister. My heartiest congratulations. And so, we now have ten socialist Cabinet Ministers in the world. Things are moving. Best wishes."

Things are indeed moving. The Second International is rapidly moving—towards complete merger with national-liberal politics. Quoting this telegram, the Chemnitz *Volksstimme*, militant organ of the extreme German opportunists and social-chauvinists, remarks, somewhat venomously: "The Secretary of the International Socialist Bureau unreservedly welcomes the acceptance by a Social-Democrat of a ministerial post. And yet only shortly before the war all party congresses, and international congresses, expressed sharp opposition to this! Times and views change—on this issue as on others."

The Heilmanns, Davids and Südekums are quite justified in their condescending praise of the Huysmans, Plekhanovs and Vanderveldes.

Stauning recently published a letter he wrote to Vandervelde. It is full of the stinging remarks a pro-German social-chauvinist would write about a French social-chauvinist. Among other things, Stauning boasts of the fact that "we [the Danish Party] have sharply and definitely disassociated ourselves from the organisationally pernicious splitting activities conducted on the initiative of the Italian and Swiss parties under the name of the Zimmerwald movement." This is literally what he says!

The formation of a national state in Denmark dates back to the sixteenth century. The masses of the Danish people passed through the bourgeois liberation movement long ago. More than 96 per cent of the population are Danes. The number of Danes in Germany is less than two hundred thousand. (The population of Denmark is 2,900,000.) This alone proves what a crude bourgeois deception is the talk of the Danish bourgeoisie about an "independent national state" being the task of the day! This is being said in the twentieth century by the bourgeoisie and the monarchists of Denmark, who *possess colonies* with a population nearly equal to the number of Danes in Germany, and over which the Danish Government is trying to *strike a bargain.*

Who says that in our day there is no trade in human beings? There is quite a brisk trade. Denmark is selling to America for so many millions (not yet agreed upon) three islands, all populated, of course.

In addition, a specific feature of Danish imperialism is the superprofits it obtains from its monopolistically advantageous position in the meat and dairy produce market: using cheap maritime transport, she supplies the world's biggest market, London. As a result, the Danish bourgeoisie and the rich Danish peasants (bourgeois of the purest type, in spite of the fables of the Russian Narodniks) have become "prosperous" satellites of the British imperialist bourgeoisie, sharing their particularly easy and particularly fat profits.

155

The Danish "Social-Democratic" Party completely succumbed to this international situation, and staunchly supported and supports the Right wing, the opportunists in the German Social-Democratic Party. The Danish Social-Democrats voted credits for the bourgeois-monarchist government to "preserve neutrality"—that was the euphemistic formula. At the Congress of September 30, 1916, there was a nine-tenths majority in favour of joining the Cabinet, in favour of a deal with the government! The correspondent of the Berne socialist paper reports that the opposition to ministerialism in Denmark was represented by Gerson Trier and the editor J. P. Sundbo. Trier defended revolutionary Marxist views in a splendid speech, and when the party decided to go into the government, he resigned from the Central Committee and from the party, declaring that he would not be a member of a *bourgeois* party. In the past few years the Danish "Social-Democratic" Party has in no way differed from the bourgeois radicals.

Greetings to Comrade G. Trier! "Things are moving," Huysmans is right—moving towards a precise, clear, politically honest, socialistically necessary division between the revolutionary Marxists, the representatives of the *masses* of the revolutionary proletariat, and the Plekhanov-Potresov-Huysmans allies and agents of the imperialist bourgeoisie, who have the majority of the *"leaders,"* but who represent the interests, not of the oppressed masses, but of the minority of privileged workers, who are deserting to the side of the bourgeoisie.

Will the Russian class-conscious workers, those who elected the deputies now exiled to Siberia, those who voted against participation in the war industries committees to support the imperialist war, wish to remain in the "International" of the *ten* Cabinet Ministers? In the International of the *Staunings*? In the International which men like *Trier* are leaving?

Lenin Collected Works, Vol. 23, pp. 134–136

The exploitation of worse paid labour from backward countries is particularly characteristic of imperialism. On this exploitation rests, to a certain degree, the parasitism of rich imperialist countries which bribe a part of their workers with higher wages while shamelessly and unre-strainedly exploiting the labour of "cheap" foreign workers. The words "worse paid" should be added and also the words "and frequently deprived of rights"; for the exploiters in "civilised" countries always take advantage of the fact that the imported foreign workers have no rights.

Revision of the Party Programme

Written October 6–8, 1917. First published in October 1917 in the journal Prosveshcheniye *No. 1–2.*

VI

Having thus concluded our analysis of Comrade Sokolnikov's draft, we must note one very valuable addition which he proposes and which in my opinion should be adopted and even developed. To the paragraph which deals with technical progress and the greater employment of female and child labour, he proposes to add the phrase "as well as the labour of unskilled foreign workers imported from backward countries." This addition is valuable and necessary. The exploitation of *worse paid* labour from backward countries is particularly characteristic of imperialism. On this exploitation rests, to a certain degree, the *parasitism* of rich imperialist countries which bribe a part of their workers with higher wages while shamelessly and unrestrainedly exploiting the labour of "cheap" foreign workers. The words "worse paid" should be added and also the words "and frequently deprived of rights"; for the exploiters in "civilised" countries always take advantage of the fact that the imported foreign workers have no rights. This is often to be seen in Germany in respect of workers imported from Russia; in Switzerland, of Italians; in France, of Spaniards and Italians, etc.

It would be expedient, perhaps, to emphasise more strongly and to express more vividly in our programme the prominence of the handful of the richest imperialist countries which prosper parasitically by robbing colonies and weaker nations. This is an extremely important feature of imperialism. To a certain extent it facilitates the rise of powerful revolutionary movements in countries that are subjected to imperialist plunder, and are in danger of being crushed and partitioned by the giant imperialists (such as Russia), and on the other hand, tends to a certain extent to prevent the rise of profound revolutionary movements in the countries that plunder, by imperialist methods, many colonies and foreign lands, and thus make a very large (comparatively) portion of their population *participants* in the division of the imperialist loot.

I would therefore suggest that the point on this exploitation of a number of weak countries by the richest should be inserted in that section of my draft where social-chauvinism is described. The relevant passage in the draft would then assume the following form (the additions are in italics):

Such a perversion is, on the one hand, the social-chauvinist trend, socialism in word and chauvinism in deed, the use of the "defence of the fatherland" slogan to hide the predatory interests "their own" national bourgeoisie *pursues in an imperialist war and to maintain the privileged position of citizens of rich nations which make enormous profits by pillaging colonies and weak nations.* Another such perversion, on the other hand, is the equally wide and international movement of the "Centre," etc.

Lenin Collected Works, Vol. 26, pp. 168–169

Fourth Conference of Trade Unions and Factory Committees of Moscow

Held from June 27–July 2, 1918. Full report published in 1918.

2. Reply to the Debate on the Current Situation, June 28, 1918.

… A question has been sent to me in writing; it reads as follows: "Why are counter-revolutionary newspapers still published?" One of the reasons is that there are elements among the printers who are bribed by the bourgeoisie. (Commotion, shouts: "It's not true.") You can shout as much as you like, but you will not prevent me from telling the truth, which all the workers know and which I have just begun to explain. When a worker attaches great importance to the wages he gets for working for the bourgeois press, when he says: "I want to keep my high wages by helping the bourgeoisie to sell poison, to poison the minds of the people," then I say it is as if these workers were bribed by the bourgeoisie (applause), not in the sense that any individual person was hired, but in the sense in which all Marxists have spoken about the British workers who ally themselves with their capitalists. All of you who have read trade union literature know that there are not only trade unions in Britain, but also alliances between the workers and capitalists in a particular industry for the purpose of raising prices and of robbing everybody else. All Marxists, all socialists of all countries point the finger of scorn at these cases and, beginning with Marx and Engels, say that there are workers who, owing to their ignorance and pursuit of their craft interests, allow themselves to be bribed by the bourgeoisie. They have sold their birthright, their right to

161

the socialist revolution, by entering into an alliance with their capitalists against the overwhelming majority of the workers and the
oppressed toilers in their own country, against their own class. The
same thing is happening here. When certain groups of workers say,
the fact that the stuff we print is opium, poison, spreads lies and
provocation, has nothing to do with us, we get high wages and we
don't care a hang for anybody else—we will denounce such workers. In our literature we have always said openly: "Such workers
are abandoning the working class and deserting to the side of the
bourgeoisie." (Applause.)

Lenin Collected Works, Vol. 27, pp. 484–485

Session of the Petrograd Soviet

Written March 12, 1919. First published in the Fourth (Russian) Edition of the Collected Works.

2. Replies to Written Questions.

... The other unclear note contains the following. What is to be done when workers, misled by the appeals of the Socialist-Revolutionaries, do not work, go on strike, and come out against Soviet power because of the food shortage? I cannot, of course, count on all workers, down to the last, supporting Soviet power. When the Paris workers revolted in 1871, quite a large number of workers in other towns fought against them in the whiteguard troops and crushed the Paris workers. That did not prevent politically-conscious socialists from asserting that the Paris Communards represented the entire proletariat, that is, all that was best and honest—only backward sections of the workers served in the whiteguard troops. We, too, have backward workers who are not politically conscious and who have not yet understood Soviet power; we are doing our best to enlighten them. No other government has satisfied the demands for standing representative bodies of workers to the extent the Soviets have, which are willing to give any representative of a factory a place in a government institution. We are, as far as possible, drawing workers into the implementation of the policy of the state; under capitalism, even in republics, the workers were kept out of it but Soviet power does its best to attract workers, although some of them will feel the attraction of the old for quite a long time to come.

There are very few people among you, probably only an individual or two, who remember serfdom; only very old people can remember that, but there are people who remember what things were like thirty or forty years ago. Anyone who was in the rural districts knows that some thirty years ago there were quite a number of old people in the villages who said, "It was better under serfdom, there was more order, things were strict and the women did not dress extravagantly." If you now read Gleb Uspensky—we are erecting a monument to him as one of the best writers about peasant life—you will find descriptions dating back to the eighties and nineties of honest old peasants and sometimes just ordinary elderly people who said frankly that it had been better under serfdom. When an old social order is destroyed it cannot be

Anyone who was in the rural districts knows that some thirty years ago there were quite a number of old people in the villages who said, "It was better under serfdom, there was more order, things were strict and the women did not dress extravagantly." ... When an old social order is destroyed it cannot be destroyed immediately in the minds of all people, there will always be some who are drawn to the old.

destroyed immediately in the minds of all people, there will always be some who are drawn to the old.

Some workers, printers, for instance, say that capitalism was good, there were a lot of newspapers whereas now there are few, in those days they earned a decent wage and they do not want any socialism. There were quite a number of branches of industry that depended on the rich classes or on the production of articles of luxury. Under capitalism quite a number of workers in big cities lived by producing articles of luxury. In the Soviet Republic we shall have to leave these workers unemployed for a time. We shall say to them, "Get down to some other, useful work." And the worker will say, "I did delicate work, I was a jeweler, it was clean work, I worked for gentlemen; now the muzhik is in power, the gentlemen have been scattered and I want to go back to capitalism." Such people will preach going back to capitalism, or, as the Mensheviks say, going forward to healthy capitalism and sound democracy. A few hundred workers are to be found who will say, "We lived well under a healthy capitalism." The people who lived well under capitalism were an insignificant minority—we defend the interests of the majority that lived badly under capitalism. (Applause.) Healthy capitalism led to world slaughter in the countries with the greatest freedom. There can be no healthy capitalism, there can be capitalism of the sort obtaining in the freest republic, one like the American republic, cultured, rich, technically developed; and that democratic and most republican capitalism, led to the most savage world slaughter over the plunder of the whole world. Out of fifteen million workers you will find a few thousand who lived well under capitalism. In the rich countries there are more such workers because they work for a greater number of millionaires and multimillionaires. They served that handful and received particularly high wages from them. Take hundreds of British millionaires—they have accumulated thousands of millions because they have plundered India and a large number of colonies. It meant nothing to them to make gifts to 10,000 or 20,000 workers, giving them double or higher wages so that they would work well for them. I once read the reminiscences of an American barber whom a multimillionaire paid a dollar a day to shave him. And that barber wrote a whole book praising that multimillionaire and his own wonderful life. For a daily visit of one hour to his financial majesty he received a dollar, was satisfied and did not want anything but capitalism. We have to be on our guard against such an argument. The vast majority of workers were not in such a position. We, the Communists of the whole world, defend the interests of the vast majority of working people, and it was a small minority of working people whom the capitalists bribed with high wages and made them the loyal servants of capital. Under serfdom there were people, peasants, who said to the landowners, "We are your slaves [that was after emancipation], we shall not leave you." Were there many of them? An insignificant few. Can you deny that there was a struggle against serfdom by reference to them? Of course not. And today communism cannot be denied by reference to the minority of workers who earned good money on bourgeois newspapers, on the production of articles of luxury and for their personal services to multimillionaires.

Lenin Collected Works, Vol. 29, pp. 27–30

The Third International and its Place in History

Written April 15, 1919. First published in May 1919.

... If any Marxist, or any person, indeed, who has a general knowledge of modern science, were asked whether it is likely that the transition of the different capitalist countries to the dictatorship of the proletariat will take place in an identical or harmoniously proportionate way, his answer would undoubtedly be in the negative. There never has been and never could be even, harmonious, or proportionate development in the capitalist world. Each country has developed more strongly first one, then another aspect or feature or group of features of capitalism and of the working-class movement. The process of development has been uneven.

When France was carrying out her great bourgeois revolution and rousing the whole European continent to a historically new life, Britain proved to be at the head of the counter-revolutionary coalition, although at the same time she was much more developed capitalistically than France. The British working-class movement of that period, however, brilliantly anticipated much that was contained in the future Marxism.

When Britain gave the world Chartism, the first broad, truly mass and politically organised proletarian revolutionary movement, bourgeois revolutions, most of them weak, were taking place on the European continent, and the first great civil war between the proletariat and the bourgeoisie had broken out in France. The bourgeoisie defeated the various national contingents of the proletariat one by one, in different ways in different countries.

Britain was the model of a country in which, as Engels put

167

it, the bourgeoisie had produced, alongside a bourgeois aristocracy, a very bourgeois upper stratum of the proletariat. For several decades this advanced capitalist country lagged behind in the
revolutionary struggle of the proletariat. France seemed to have
exhausted the strength of the proletariat in two heroic working-
class revolts of 1848 and 1871 against the bourgeoisie that made
very considerable contributions to world-historical development.
Leadership in the International of the working-class movement
then passed to Germany; that was in the seventies of the nineteenth century, when she lagged economically behind Britain and
France. But when Germany had outstripped these two countries
economically, i.e., by the second decade of the twentieth century,
the Marxist workers' party of Germany, that model for the whole
world, found itself headed by a handful of utter scoundrels, the
most filthy blackguards—from Scheidemann and Noske to David
and Legien—loathsome hangmen drawn from the workers' ranks
who had sold themselves to the capitalists, who were in the service
of the monarchy and the counter-revolutionary bourgeoisie.

World history is leading unswervingly towards the dictatorship
of the proletariat, but is doing so by paths that are anything but
smooth, simple and straight.

When Karl Kautsky was still a Marxist and not the renegade
from Marxism he became when he began to champion unity with
the Scheidemanns and to support bourgeois democracy against
Soviet, or proletarian, democracy, he wrote an article—this was
at the turn of the century—entitled "The Slavs and Revolution."
In this article he traced the historical conditions that pointed to
the possibility of leadership in the world revolutionary movement

passing to the Slavs.

And so it has. Leadership in the revolutionary proletarian International has passed for a time—for a short time, it goes without saying—to the Russians, just as at various periods of the nineteenth century it was in the hands of the British, then of the French, then of the Germans.

I have had occasion more than once to say that it was easier for the Russians than for the advanced countries *to begin* the great proletarian revolution, but that it will be more difficult for them *to continue* it and carry it to final victory, in the sense of the complete organisation of a socialist society.

Lenin Collected Works, Vol. 29, pp. 308–310

World history is leading unswervingly towards the dictatorship of the proletariat, but is doing so by paths that are anything but smooth, simple and straight.

The Tasks of the Third International: Ramsay Macdonald on the Third International

Written July 14, 1919. First published August 1919.

III

Ramsay MacDonald, with the amusing naiveté of a "drawing-room" socialist who carelessly uses words without at all understanding their serious significance, giving no thought whatever to the fact that *words commit one to deeds*, declares that in Berne "a concession to non-socialist public opinion" was made.

Precisely! We regard the whole of the Berne International as yellow, treacherous and perfidious because the *whole* of its policy is a *"concession"* to the bourgeoisie.

Ramsay MacDonald knows perfectly well that we have built the Third International and broken unreservedly with the Second International because we became convinced that it was hopeless, incorrigible, played the part of a servant to imperialism, of a vehicle of bourgeois influence, bourgeois lies and bourgeois corruption in the labour movement. If in desiring to

For the proletariat needs the truth, and there is nothing more harmful to its cause than plausible, respectable, petty-bourgeois lies.

discuss the Third International Ramsay MacDonald evades the substance of the matter, beats about the bush, utters empty phrases and does not speak of what should be spoken about, that is his fault and his crime. For the proletariat needs the truth, and there is nothing more harmful to its cause than plausible, respectable, petty-bourgeois lies.

The problem of imperialism and of *its connection* with opportunism in the labour movement, with the betrayal of the workers' cause by labour leaders, was raised long ago, very long ago.

For a period of *forty* years, from 1852 to 1892, Marx and Engels constantly pointed to the fact that the upper stratum of the British working class was becoming increasingly *bourgeois* as a consequence of the country's peculiar economic conditions (colonies, monopoly of the world market, etc.). In the seventies of last century Marx won himself the honourable hatred of the despicable heroes of the Berne International trend of those days, of the opportunists and reformists, for branding many of the British trade union leaders as men who had sold themselves to the bourgeoisie or were in its pay for services rendered to *its* class *from within* the labour movement.

During the Anglo–Boer War, the Anglo-Saxon press quite clearly raised the problem of imperialism as the latest *(and last)* stage of capitalism. If my memory serves me right, it was none other than Ramsay MacDonald who then resigned from the Fabian Society, that prototype of the Berne International, that nursery and model of opportunism, which Engels describes, with the power, brilliancy and truth of genius, in his correspondence with Sorge. "Fabian imperialism"—such was the common expression employed at that time in British socialist literature.

171

If Ramsay MacDonald has forgotten this, all the worse for him.

"Fabian imperialism" and "social-imperialism" are one and the same thing: socialism in words, imperialism in deeds, *the growth of opportunism into imperialism*. This has now become, during the war of 1914–18 and since, a universal fact. The failure to understand it shows the great blindness of the Berne yellow International, and is its great crime. Opportunism, or reformism, inevitably had to grow into a phenomenon of world-wide importance, *socialist imperialism*, or social-chauvinism, because imperialism brought to the fore a handful of very rich, advanced nations, engaged in plundering the whole world, and thereby enabled the bourgeoisie of those countries, out of their monopolist superprofits (imperialism is monopoly capitalism), *to bribe the upper strata of the working class.*

Only ignoramuses or hypocrites who deceive the workers by repeating *platitudes* about capitalism and in this way cover up the bitter truth that *a whole trend in socialism* has gone over to the imperialist bourgeoisie could fail to see the economic inevitability of this development under imperialism.

And from this fact two indisputable conclusions emerge.

First conclusion: the Berne International is in fact, from the angle of its real historical and political role, and irrespective of the good will and pious wishes of particular members of it, *an organisation of agents of international imperialism* operating *within* the labour movement, permeating *that movement* with bourgeois influence, bourgeois ideas, bourgeois lies, and bourgeois corruption.

In countries where democratic parliamentary culture is of long standing, the bourgeoisie has learned splendidly to use deception, bribery and flattery in their most subtle forms as well as violence.

172

Not for nothing have the "luncheons" given to British "labour leaders" (i.e., lieutenants of the bourgeoisie whose duty is to fool the workers) have acquired notoriety; Engels in his day spoke about them. To the same category of facts belongs the "charming" reception given by M. Clemenceau to the traitor-socialist Merrheim, the courteous receptions given by Entente ministers to the leaders of the Berne International, and so on and so forth. "You train 'em, and we buy 'em," a clever capitalist, an Englishwoman, said to Mr. Social-imperialist Hyndman, who related in his memoirs how this lady, a person shrewder than all the leaders of the Berne International put together, appraised the "labours" of the socialist intellectuals in training workers to become socialist leaders.

During the war, when the Vanderveldes, Brantings and the whole gang of traitors organised "international" conferences, the French bourgeois newspapers were bitingly scornful, and rightly so. They said: "These Vanderveldes seem to be suffering from a sort of tic. Just as those who suffer from tic cannot utter a couple of phrases without strangely twitching the muscles of the face, so the Vanderveldes cannot make a political speech without repeating, parrot-like, the words internationalism, socialism, international working-class solidarity, proletarian revolution, etc. Let them repeat any sacramental formulas they like so long as they help to lead the workers by the nose and serve us, the capitalists, in waging the imperialist war and enslaving the workers."

Sometimes the British and French bourgeoisie are very clever and excellently appraise the servile role played by the Berne International. ...

IV

... In order to really defeat opportunism, which caused the shameful death of the Second International, in order to really assist the revolution, the approach of which *even* Ramsay MacDonald is obliged to admit, it is necessary:

Firstly, to conduct all propaganda and agitation from the viewpoint of revolution as opposed to reforms, systematically explaining to the masses, both theoretically and practically, at every step of parliamentary, trade union, co-operative, etc., activity, that they are diametrically opposed. Under no circumstances to refrain (save in special cases, by way of exception) from utilising the parliamentary system and all the "liberties" of bourgeois democracy; not to reject reforms, but to regard them *only* as a *by-product* of the revolutionary class struggle of the proletariat. Not a single party affiliated to the Berne International meets these requirements. Not a single one of them shows that it has any idea of how to conduct its propaganda and agitation *as a whole*, explaining how reform *differs* from revolution; nor do they know how to train both the Party and the masses *unswervingly for revolution.*

...

Fourthly, there must be no toleration of the verbal condemnation of imperialism while no real revolutionary struggle is waged for the liberation of the colonies (and dependent nations) from one's *own* imperialist bourgeoisie. That is hypocrisy. That is the policy of the agents of the bourgeoisie in the labour movement (labour lieutenants of the capitalist class). The British, French, Dutch, Belgian, or other party which is hostile to imperialism in words but in deeds does not wage a revolutionary struggle within "its own" colonies for the *overthrow* of "its own" bourgeoisie, does not systematically assist the *revolutionary* work which has already begun everywhere in the colonies, and does not send arms and literature to the revolutionary parties in the colonies, is a party of scoundrels and traitors.

Lenin Collected Works, Vol. 29, pp. 500–503, 504, 505–506

> The British, French, Dutch, Belgian, or other party which is hostile to imperialism in words but in deeds does not wage a revolutionary struggle within "its own" colonies for the overthrow of "its own" bourgeoisie, does not systematically assist the revolutionary work which has already begun everywhere in the colonies, and does not send arms and literature to the revolutionary parties in the colonies, is a party of scoundrels and traitors.

Without the exposure of this evil, without a struggle against both the trade union bureaucracy and all manifestations of petty-bourgeois guildism, against the working-class aristocracy, the privileges of the upper stratum of workers, without the ruthless removal from the revolutionary party of those imbued with this spirit, without an appeal to the lower strata, to ever wider sections of the masses, to the real majority of the exploited—without all this there can be no question of the dictatorship of the proletariat.

Draft (or Theses) of the R.C.P.'s Reply to the Letter of the Independent Social-Democratic Party of Germany

Published in March 1920.

...

10. Every revolution (as distinguished from a reform) by its very nature implies a crisis, and a very deep crisis at that, both political and economic. This is irrespective of the crisis brought about by the war.

It is the task of the revolutionary party of the proletariat to explain to the workers and peasants that they must have the courage to meet this crisis boldly and find in revolutionary measures a *source of strength* with which to overcome the crisis. Only by surmounting the greatest crises with revolutionary enthusiasm, with revolutionary energy, with revolutionary preparedness to make the greatest sacrifices, can the proletariat defeat the exploiters and liberate mankind entirely from wars, the oppression of capital and wage-slavery.

There is no other way, because the reformist attitude to capitalism yesterday engendered the imperialist bloodbath (and will certainly do the same tomorrow) involving millions of people and endless crises.

This is the main idea without which the dictatorship of the proletariat is an empty phrase; the Independents and the Longuetists do not understand it and do not include it in their agitation and propaganda, do not explain it to the masses.

...

13. The Independents and the Longuetists do not understand and do not explain to the masses that the imperialist superprofits of the advanced countries enabled them (and still enable them) to *bribe* the top stratum of the proletariat, to throw them some crumbs from the superprofits (obtained from the colonies and from the financial exploitation of weak countries), to create a privileged section of skilled workers, etc.

Without the exposure of this evil, without a struggle against both the trade union bureaucracy and all manifestations of petty-bourgeois guildism, against the working-class aristocracy, the privileges of the upper stratum of workers, without the ruthless removal from the revolutionary party of those imbued with this spirit, without an appeal to the lower strata, to ever wider sections of the masses, to the real *majority of the exploited*—without all this there can be no question of the dictatorship of the proletariat.

14. This unwillingness or inability to break with the top stratum of workers who are infected with imperialism, is also found among the Independents and the Longuetists in their not conducting agitation for the direct, unqualified support for all insurrections and revolutionary movements of *colonial* peoples.

Under such circumstances the condemnation of colonial policy and of imperialism is either sheer hypocrisy or the empty sighing of a stupid philistine. ...

Lenin Collected Works, Vol. 30, pp. 341–343

"Left-Wing" Communism—An Infantile Disorder

Written in April–May 1920. Published in pamphlet form in June 1920.

... Further. In countries more advanced than Russia, a certain reactionism in the trade unions has been and was bound to be manifested in a far greater measure than in our country. Our Mensheviks found support in the trade unions (and to some extent still do so in a small number of unions), as a result of the latter's craft narrow-mindedness, craft selfishness and opportunism. The Mensheviks of the West have acquired a much firmer footing in the trade unions; there the *craft-union, narrow-minded, selfish, case-hardened, covetous, and petty-bourgeois "labour aristocracy," imperialist-minded, and imperialist-corrupted*, has developed into a much stronger section than in our country. That is incontestable. The struggle against the Gomperses, and against the Jouhaux, Hendersons, Merrheims, Legiens and Co. in Western Europe is much more difficult than the struggle against our Mensheviks, who are an *absolutely homogeneous* social and political type. This struggle must be waged ruthlessly, and it must unfailingly be brought—as we brought it—to a point when all the incorrigible leaders of opportunism and social-chauvinism are completely discredited and driven out of the trade unions. Political power cannot be captured (and the attempt to capture it should not be made) until the struggle has reached a *certain* stage. This "certain stage" will be *different* in different countries and in different circumstances; it can be correctly gauged only by thoughtful, experienced and knowledgeable political leaders of the proletariat in each particular country. ...

Lenin Collected Works, Vol. 31, pp. 51–52

The Second Congress of the Communist International

The Second Congress of the Communist International took place from July 19–August 7, 1920. First published in full in 1921 in the book The Second Congress of the Communist International. Verbatim Report.

1. Report on the International Situation and the Fundamental Tasks of the Communist International. July 19.

... Here we must ask: how is the persistence of such trends in Europe to be explained? Why is this opportunism stronger in Western Europe than in our country? It is because the culture of the advanced countries has been, and still is, the result of their being able to live at the expense of a thousand million oppressed people. It is because the capitalists of these countries obtain a great deal more in this way than they could obtain as profits by plundering the workers in their own countries.

Before the war, it was calculated that the three richest countries—Britain, France and Germany—got between eight and ten thousand million francs a year from the export of capital alone, apart from other sources.

It goes without saying that, out of this tidy sum, at least five hundred millions can be spent as a sop to the labour leaders and the labour aristocracy, i.e., on all sorts of bribes. The whole thing boils down to nothing but bribery. It is done in a thousand different ways: by increasing cultural facilities in the largest centres, by creating educational institutions, and by providing co-operative, trade union and parliamentary leaders with thousands of cushy jobs. This is done wherever present-day civilised capitalist relations exist. It is these thousands of millions in superprofits that form the economic basis of opportunism in the working-class movement. In America, Britain and France we see a far greater persistence of the opportunist leaders, of the upper crust of the working class, the labour aristocracy; they offer stronger resistance to the Communist movement. That is why we must be prepared to find it harder for the European and American workers' parties to get rid of this disease than was the case in our country. We know that enormous successes have been achieved in the treatment of this disease since the Third International was formed, but we have not yet finished the job; the purging of the workers' parties, the revolutionary parties of the proletariat all over the world, of bourgeois influences, of the opportunists in their ranks, is very far from complete.

I shall not dwell on the concrete manner in which we must do that; that is dealt with in my published theses. My task consists in indicating the deep economic roots of this phenomenon. The disease is a protracted one; the cure takes longer than the optimists hoped it would. Opportunism is our principal enemy. Opportunism in the upper ranks of the working-class movement is bourgeois socialism, not proletarian socialism. It has been shown in practice that working-class activists who follow the opportunist trend are better defenders of the bourgeoisie than the bourgeois themselves. Without their leadership of the workers, the bourgeoisie could not remain in power. This has been proved, not only by the history of the Kerensky regime in Russia; it has also been proved by the democratic republic in Germany under its Social-Democratic government, as well as by Albert Thomas's attitude towards his bourgeois government. It has been proved by similar experience in Britain and the United States. This is where our principal enemy is, an enemy we must overcome. We must leave this Congress firmly resolved to carry on this struggle to the very end, in all parties. That is our main task. ...

Opportunism is our principal enemy. Opportunism in the upper ranks of the working-class movement is bourgeois socialism, not proletarian socialism. It has been shown in practice that working-class activists who follow the opportunist trend are better defenders of the bourgeoisie than the bourgeois themselves. Without their leadership of the workers, the bourgeoisie could not remain in power.

3. Report of the Commission on the National and the Colonial Questions. July 26.

... I would also like to emphasise the importance of revolutionary work by the Communist parties, not only in their own, but also in the colonial countries, and particularly among the troops employed by the exploiting nations to keep the colonial peoples in subjection.

Comrade Quelch of the British Socialist Party spoke of this in our commission. He said that the rank-and-file British worker would consider it treasonable to help the enslaved nations in their uprisings against British rule. True, the jingoist and chauvinist-minded labour aristocrats of Britain and America present a very great danger to socialism, and are a bulwark of the Second International. Here we are confronted with the greatest treachery on the part of leaders and workers belonging to this bourgeois International. The colonial question has been discussed in the Second International as well. The Basle Manifesto is quite clear on this point, too. The parties of the Second International have pledged themselves to revolutionary action, but they have given no sign of genuine revolutionary work or of assistance to the exploited and dependent nations in their revolt against the oppressor nations. This, I think, applies also to most of the parties that have withdrawn from the Second International and wish to join the Third International. We must proclaim this publicly for all to hear, and it is irrefutable. We shall see if any attempt is made to deny it. ...

Lenin Collected Works, Vol. 31, pp. 230–231, 245

4. Speech on the Terms of Admission into the Communist International. July 30.

… Then Crispien went on to speak of high wages. The position in Germany, he said, is that the workers are quite well off compared with the workers in Russia or in general, in the East of Europe. A revolution, as he sees it, can be made only if it does not worsen the workers' conditions "too much." Is it permissible, in a Communist Party, to speak in a tone like this, I ask? This is the language of counter-revolution. The standard of living in Russia in undoubtedly lower than in Germany, and when we established the dictatorship, this led to the workers beginning to go more hungry and to their conditions becoming even worse. The workers' victory cannot be achieved without sacrifices, without a temporary deterioration of their conditions. We must tell the workers the very opposite of what Crispien has said. If, in desiring to prepare the workers for the dictatorship, one tells them that their conditions will not be worsened "too much," one is losing sight of the main thing, namely, that it was by helping their "own" bourgeoisie to conquer and strangle the whole world by imperialist methods, with the aim of thereby ensuring better pay for themselves, that the labour aristocracy developed. If the German workers now want to work for the revolution they must make sacrifices, and not be afraid to do so.

In the general and world-historical sense, it is true that in a backward country like China, the coolie cannot bring about a proletarian revolution; however to tell the workers in the handful of rich countries where life is easier, thanks to imperialist pillage, that they must be afraid of "too great" impoverishment, is counter-revolutionary. It is the reverse that they should be told. The labour aristocracy that is afraid of sacrifices, afraid of "too great" impoverishment during the revolutionary struggle, cannot belong to the Party. Otherwise the dictatorship is impossible, especially in West-European countries. ...

Lenin Collected Works, Vol. 31, pp. 248–249

The workers' victory cannot be achieved without sacrifices, without a temporary deterioration of their conditions. We must tell the workers the very opposite of what Crispien has said. If, in desiring to prepare the workers for the dictatorship, one tells them that their conditions will not be worsened "too much," one is losing sight of the main thing, namely, that it was by helping their "own" bourgeoisie to conquer and strangle the whole world by imperialist methods, with the aim of thereby ensuring better pay for themselves, that the labour aristocracy developed.

6. Speech on Affiliation to the British Labour Party. August 6.

... The comrades have emphasised that the labour aristocracy is stronger in Britain than in any other country. That is true. After all, the labour aristocracy has existed in Britain, not for decades but for centuries. The British bourgeoisie, which has had far more experience—democratic experience—than that of any other country, has been able to buy workers over and to create among them a sizable stratum, greater than in any other country, but one that is not so great compared with the masses of the workers. This stratum is thoroughly imbued with bourgeois prejudices and pursues a definitely bourgeois reformist policy. In Ireland, for instance, there are two hundred thousand British soldiers who are applying ferocious terror methods to suppress the Irish. The British Socialists are not conducting any revolutionary propaganda among these soldiers, though our resolutions clearly state that we can accept into the Communist International only those British parties that conduct genuinely revolutionary propaganda among the British workers and soldiers. I emphasise that we have heard no objections to this either here or in the commissions. ...

Lenin Collected Works, Vol. 31, p. 261

Better Fewer, But Better

Written on March 2, 1923. First published March 4, 1923 in Pravda
No. 49.

... The system of international relationships which has now taken
shape is one in which a European state, Germany, is enslaved by the
victor countries. Furthermore, owing to their victory, a number of
states, the oldest states in the West, are in a position to make some
insignificant concessions to their oppressed classes—concessions
which, insignificant though they are, nevertheless retard the revolutionary movement in those countries and create some semblance
of "class truce."

At the same time, as a result of the last imperialist war, a
number of countries of the East, India, China, etc., have been
completely jolted out of the rut. Their development has definitely
shifted to general European capitalist lines. The general European
ferment has begun to affect them, and it is now clear to the whole
world that they have been drawn into a process of development that
must lead to a crisis in the whole of world capitalism.

Thus, at the present time we are confronted with the question—shall we be able to hold on with our small and very small
peasant production, and in our present state of ruin, until the
West-European capitalist countries consummate their development towards socialism? But they are consummating it not as we
formerly expected. They are not consummating it through the
gradual "maturing" of socialism, but through the exploitation of
some countries by others, through the exploitation of the first of
the countries vanquished in the imperialist war combined with the

exploitation of the whole of the East. On the other hand, precisely as a result of the first imperialist war, the East has been definitely drawn into the revolutionary movement, has been definitely drawn into the general maelstrom of the world revolutionary movement.

What tactics does this situation prescribe for our country? Obviously the following. We must display extreme caution so as to preserve our workers' government and to retain our small and very small peasantry under its leadership and authority. We have the advantage that the whole world is now passing to a movement that must give rise to a world socialist revolution. But we are labouring under the disadvantage that the imperialists have succeeded in splitting the world into two camps; and this split is made more complicated by the fact that it is extremely difficult for Germany, which is really a land of advanced, cultured, capitalist development, to rise to her feet. All the capitalist powers of what is called the West are pecking at her and preventing her from rising. On the other hand, the entire East, with its hundreds of millions of exploited working people, reduced to the last degree of human suffering, has been forced into a position where its physical and material strength cannot possibly be compared with the physical, material and military strength of any of the much smaller West-European states.

Can we save ourselves from the impending conflict with these imperialist countries? May we hope that the internal antagonisms and conflicts between the thriving imperialist countries of the West and the thriving imperialist countries of the East will give us a second respite as they did the first time, when the campaign of the West-European counter-revolution in support of the Russian counter-revolution broke down owing to the antagonisms in the camp of the counter-revolutionaries of the West and the East, in the camp of the Eastern and Western exploiters, in the camp of Japan and the U.S.A.?

I think the reply to this question should be that the issue depends upon too many factors, and that the outcome of the struggle as a whole can be forecast only because in the long run capitalism itself is educating and training the vast majority of the population of the globe for the struggle.

In the last analysis, the outcome of the struggle will be determined by the fact that Russia, India, China, etc., account for the overwhelming majority of the population of the globe. And during the past few years it is this majority that has been drawn into the struggle for emancipation with extraordinary rapidity, so that in this respect there cannot be the slightest doubt what the final outcome of the world struggle will be. In this sense, the complete victory of socialism is fully and absolutely assured. ...

Lenin Collected Works, Vol. 33, pp. 498–500

Neither we nor anyone else can calculate precisely what portion of the proletariat is following and will follow the social-chauvinists and opportunists. This will be revealed only by the struggle, it will be definitely decided only by the socialist revolution. But we know for certain that the "defenders of the fatherland" in the imperialist war represent only a minority. And it is therefore our duty, if we wish to remain socialists, to go down lower and deeper, to the real masses; this is the whole meaning and the whole purport of the struggle against opportunism. By exposing the fact that the opportunists and social-chauvinists are in reality betraying and selling the interests of the masses, that they are defending the temporary privileges of a minority of the workers, that they are the vehicles of bourgeois ideas and influences, that they are really allies and agents of the bourgeoisie, we teach the masses to appreciate their true political interests, to fight for socialism and for the revolution through all the long and painful vicissitudes of imperialist wars and imperialist armistices.

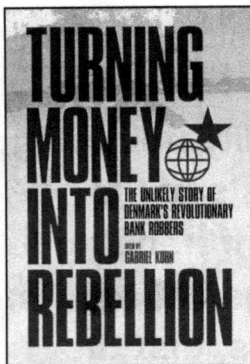

Turning Money into Rebellion: The Unlikely Story of Denmark's Revolutionary Bank Robbers

ed. Gabriel Kuhn • 978-1-60486-316-1

224 pages • $20.00

One of the most captivating chapters from the European anti-imperialist milieu of the 1970s and '80s; the Blekingegade Group had emerged from a communist organization whose analysis of the metropolitan labor aristocracy led them to develop an illegal and internationalist practice, sending millions of dollars acquired in spectacular heists to Third World liberation movements.

This book includes historical documents, illustrations, and an exclusive interview with Torkil Lauesen and Jan Weimann, two of the group's longest-standing members. It is a compelling tale of turning radical theory into action and concerns analysis and strategy as much as morality and political practice. Perhaps most importantly, it revolves around the cardinal question of revolutionary politics: What to do, and how to do it?

KERSPLEBEDEB, CP 63560, CCCP VAN HORNE, MONTREAL, QUEBEC, CANADA H3W 3H8

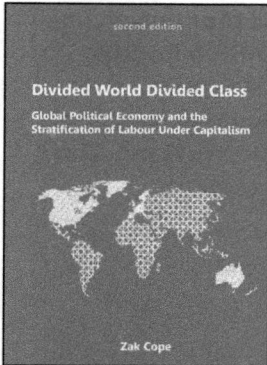

KERSPLEBEDEB, CP 63560, CCCP VAN HORNE, MONTREAL, QUEBEC, CANADA H3W 3H8

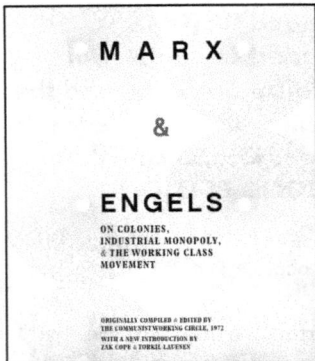

Karl Marx and Friedrich Engels: On Colonies, Industrial Monopoly, & the Working Class Movement

Introduction by Zak Cope and Torkil Lauesen

978-1-894946-79-7

160 pages • $10.00

Selections from the corpus of Marx and Engels, showing the evolution of their ideas on the nascent labor aristocracy and the complicating factors of colonialism and chauvinism, with a focus on the British Empire of their time. In their introduction, Cope and Lauesen show how Marx and Engels's initial belief that capitalism would extend seamlessly around the globe in the same form was proven wrong by events, as instead worldwide imperialism spread capitalism as a polarizing process, not only between the bourgeoisie and the working class, but also as a division between an imperialist center and an exploited periphery.

KERSPLEBEDEB, CP 63560, CCCP VAN HORNE, MONTREAL, QUEBEC, CANADA H3W 3H8

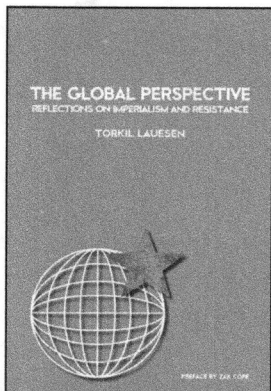

The Global Perspective: Reflections on Imperialism and Resistance

Torkil Lauesen • 978-1-894946-93-3
544 pages • $24.95

We today live in a world of massive and unprecedented inequality. Never before has humanity been so starkly divided between the "haves" and the "have nots." Never before has the global situation been accelerating so quickly. The Third World national liberation movements of the 20th century very much triggered the liberatory movements that did manage to emerge in the First World, and seemed for an all-too-brief moment to point to an escape hatch from history's downward spiral ... but for many today that all seems like ancient history.

The Global Perspective bridges the gap between Third Worldist theory, and the question of "What Is To Be Done?" in a First World context. As Lauesen says, "It is a book written by an activist, for activists. Global capitalism is heading into a deep structural crisis in the coming decades, so the objective conditions for radical change will be present, for better or for worse. The outcome will depend on us, the subjective forces."

KERSPLEBEDEB, CP 63560, CCCP VAN HORNE, MONTREAL, QUEBEC, CANADA H3W 3H8

KER SPL EBE DEB

Since 1998 Kersplebedeb has been an important source of radical literature and agit prop materials.

The project has a non-exclusive focus on anti-patriarchal and anti-imperialist politics, framed within an anticapitalist perspective. A special priority is given to writings regarding armed struggle in the metropole and the continuing struggles of political prisoners and prisoners of war.

Kersplebedeb can be contacted at:

> Kersplebedeb
> CP 63560, CCCP Van Horne
> Montreal, Quebec
> Canada H3W 3H8

> email: info@kersplebedeb.com
> web: www.kersplebedeb.com
>   www.leftwingbooks.net

Kersplebedeb

www.ingramcontent.com/pod-product-compliance
Lightning Source LLC
Chambersburg PA
CBHW060848280326
41934CB00007B/964